THE
DISCIPLINES
5
™

The 5 Disciplines
of Highly Effective
EMPLOYEES

Maximize
YOUR
Potential

Mike Fedotowsky • Seth Hummel
Mendy Fedotowsky • Lexi Ball

Printed in the United States of America

First Printing, 2017

ISBN 978-1-945091-44-5

Ordering Information: Special discounts are available on quantity purchases by bookstores, corporations, associations, and others. For details, contact the publisher at:

sales@braughlerbooks.com
or at 937-58-BOOKS

For questions or comments about this book, please write to:

info@braughlerbooks.com

Braughler™
Books
braughlerbooks.com

CONTENTS

INTRODUCTION

"With self-discipline
most anything is possible."

Theodore Roosevelt

INTRODUCTION

The 5 Disciplines purpose statement is:

"To help organizations and the people who work there reach their full potential."

An organization can only reach its full potential if the people who work in it are able to reach their full potential. This can only be achieved when a person continuously improves how they perform their job each and every day.

However, this process alone cannot help an organization reach its full potential. In fact, "The 5 Disciplines of Highly Effective Employees" is part of a larger management system that includes "The 5 Disciplines of Highly Effective Managers" and "The 5 Disciplines of Highly Effective Executives." Therefore, in this book we are not going to cover topics such as leading people and strategic thinking.

It is well known that people who have achieved their full potential have a high degree of self-discipline. The 5 Disciplines offers a disciplined approach to self-improvement that can help any individual achieve their full potential regardless of job title. It applies to employees at every level, from the person just starting their career all the way to the seasoned executive.

The 5 Disciplines has its roots in the scientific method, which is a universal process that scientists use for advancing knowledge. Scientists are taught to plan an experiment, conduct the experiment, study the results, and act based upon the new information. This process of gaining knowledge has led to incredible breakthroughs in technology and productivity. Our thirst for knowledge and our ability to use it for the good of the human species has allowed us to continue making progress in our quality of life.

Using the scientific method to solve organizational problems began when Dr. W. Edwards Deming introduced the Plan, Do, Study, Act cycle for continuous improvement to Japan in the

1950s. Deming's PDSA cycle, along with his philosophy to empower employees to solve common work problems, evolved into what is now called the Lean Six Sigma five step problem-solving process.

1. Define – Define the Problem (Plan)
2. Measure – Measure the Problem (Plan)
3. Analyze – Analyze the Causes (Plan)
4. Improve – Implement Solutions (Do)
5. Control – Maintain the Gains (Study & Act)

Albert Einstein once said that "Everything should be made as simple as possible, but no simpler." The 5 Disciplines is a culmination of 75 years of consulting and learning from the brightest minds in business. This learning has been boiled down into five simple questions that follow the DMAIC process.

1. Define (Plan) – What is my job?
2. Measure (Plan) – Am I doing a good job?
3. Analyze (Plan) – How do I analyze my job?
4. Improve (Do) – How do I improve?
5. Control (Study & Act) – Am I maintaining the gains?

The systematic 5 Disciplines process provides you with a roadmap to lead you to your full potential at work and beyond.

The content of this book is broken into 5 sections, with one for each step in The 5 Disciplines. Most of each chapter narrates an Account Coordinator, Lauren, learning the step from her mentor, Claire. With the information she learns from Claire, Lauren implements the steps within her job.

At the end of each chapter, a Summary section explains the purpose of the step and lists the questions associated with it. Each Summary section asks five questions, which are designed to guide you through each step. Please note that the sub-questions in this book are chosen based on Lauren's situation, but there may be other questions to ask based on your own circumstances. The Summary section also reiterates Lauren's answer to each question during the previous step. To customize and execute each discipline, you can find helpful tools at the5disciplines.org.

The narrative portion of the book is designed to explain each discipline and illustrate how it can be executed. The Summary portion then outlines the questions needed to gather information that answers the overarching question of each step.

As with every improvement methodology, The 5 Disciplines requires a commitment to implementation. The principles included in The 5 Disciplines must be applied over time to begin truly making a difference. In the same vein as the scientific method, long-term success is about continuous improvement on a daily basis.

1

DEFINE

What is
My Job?

STEP 1: DEFINE

Lauren sat in her office at Maximum Potential, Inc. at 9am, and already knew this was going to be one of *those* days. Her inbox contained two emails. The first was an invitation to a meeting in fifteen minutes with her boss at Maximum Potential, Inc., Justin. It was a formal meeting, with Justin alone, scheduled last minute. She knew something was wrong.

The second email was from her biggest client, Symbay. Normally she communicated with Stan, who handled day-to-day operations at Symbay. She had a great working relationship with him. He was easy to work with and never seemed stressed out. But this email was from Phillip, the company's VP of Operations. She rarely heard from him. When she did, it never seemed to be good news.

Before opening the email, she ran through everything that had happened with the account in the previous week. In her new role as Account Coordinator, she had been assigned to the Symbay account. Symbay had typically been a satisfied client. They loved the MaxPTs—a tablet designed for business use that could be personalized for each employee. Lauren felt she had stable footing, but there had been some problems in recent months.

The MaxPT was the cornerstone product of Maximum Potential, Inc. It existed to help every employee reach their "Maximum Potential." The MaxPT included some of the latest innovations in machine learning. Its major selling point was that the tablet adapted to the user's style of work and learned to anticipate what each user needed to accomplish next. Symbay leadership loved that employees could have a tablet they could use anywhere. It kept all of their information in one place, kept the information secure, and customized that information to the employees' individualized needs.

With the growth of the account, customer concerns had begun slipping through the cracks. And Symbay wasn't the only client committed to using MaxPTs. In fact, just like Symbay, other key accounts had begun demanding more of the product. Sales had skyrocketed…for a while.

Recently, the MaxPTs had run into some quality issues. Maximum Potential, Inc. couldn't keep up with the sharp increase in sales and Dr. Parker, the company's founder, didn't know how to improve quality. In fact, all he seemed interested in was tinkering with his inventions and training his pit bulls. In the company, a culture had begun to develop that lacked any structure for improvement. The company looked like it was headed down a rocky path, and Lauren had an email from Phillip at Symbay to prove it.

To: Lauren

Subject: Technical Issues with MaxPTs

From: Phillip

Lauren,

I have heard numerous times over the last three months that our employees are having difficulty using the MaxPTs. We are experiencing technical issues and aren't able to seamlessly integrate the tablets into our daily operations. We can't afford to continue having issues while seeing no real, long-term solutions. The tablets are not showing the long-term value we hoped for. As a company, it may be time for us to explore other options.

Please respond with how you plan to fix this problem.

— Phillip

Lauren finished the email and was somehow out of breath. Her mind was racing through all of the moves she'd made over the past week. Could she have been more attentive? Why couldn't she fix these problems by herself? Why couldn't her boss do more to keep the peace?

The reminder for her meeting with Justin popped up on her computer and broke her train of thought.

"Oh, right. Our meeting. Crap."

She closed the meeting reminder and behind it was the email she had just read. Only now did she notice that Phillip had copied Justin on the email. Lauren suddenly knew what her meeting was about.

• • • • •

She opened the door to the conference room to find Justin sitting directly across the room, facing her. He had his MaxPT neatly arranged next to his pen, next to his phone, next to the MaxPT training manual. His posture was upright and rigid. His lips pursed like he was doing his best to hold back a lecture.

Justin seemed like a difficult person to get along with. He had his way of doing things and didn't typically open up to other employees. He used to have some of Lauren's responsibilities, but when Maximum Potential started landing bigger clients he was promoted to Director of Account Services. Now he was responsible for overseeing the Account Coordinator team, managing high level client relationships, leading device customization, and training his direct reports.

Before Lauren could sit down and log into her MaxPT for the meeting, Justin launched into a rant.

"Lauren, when you were promoted from Lead Tech Support Rep to Account Coordinator six months ago, I expected you to be able to handle the Symbay account. Now I have an email from their VP of Operations saying they aren't seeing the value in our product.

"First of all, they shouldn't have technical issues. If you manage the account correctly, things should operate smoothly and the MaxPTs should have no technical mishaps. Second, when they do have issues, we need Tech Support to fix them. Your job is to make sure the client is getting the most out of the MaxPTs and that the account relationship is on firm ground. If the client is having problems, you should be the first to know; you shouldn't be finding out in an email like this."

"Ugh!" Lauren thought. She had seen the devices set up properly and it still hadn't stopped these issues from happening, but Justin didn't seem to realize that.

Eventually Lauren caught a moment of silence to interject.

"Justin, I'm so happy to be part of this department. We have a great product and a great set of clients. But our customers had experienced technical issues long before I became an Account Coordinator. I'm working long hours to solve problems and make sure the client is happy."

Justin cut her off. "You were promoted into this position to prevent these issues from occurring, not to correct issues on the spot. You're spending too much time solving tech support issues and not enough time helping the customer use the MaxPTs correctly. You're putting out fires instead of preventing them from happening in the first place."

Justin had a point. Her job was to provide account support for the client—managing initial device setup, advising on device customization, handling updates, processing invoices, facilitating training, and checking in to continually strengthen the client relationship. It was Tech Support's job to fix technical issues. But despite Justin's requests, she often chose to pursue technical support herself, feeling like it provided valuable customer interaction that would build the relationship.

Lauren spent four and a half years in Tech Support, so solving those problems came easy. Her current position was relatively new and she felt like she was making it up as she went. She often defaulted to solving problems in the way most comfortable to her.

"I understand what you're saying, but the client is used to working with me to solve their issues. They call me and I can quickly resolve the problem. When I send it over to Tech Support, I have no way of knowing when or even if the issue gets resolved. Since I can't track those things, I'm not always comfortable sending them elsewhere."

Justin dismissed her concerns and continued speaking. Eventually, he arrived at the end of his lecture. He expressed his doubts about Lauren's ability to handle the workload and demanded she make improvements to immediately address Phillip's concerns. If she couldn't repair the relationship, Justin would have to seriously consider Lauren's future at Maximum Potential. Lauren left the meeting feeling like a complete failure.

"Am I going to have a job next week?" she wondered to herself on the stairway up to her desk.

The rest of the day was just as stressful as the beginning. From 10AM until the end of the day, Lauren felt she was running around like a chicken with its head cut off. All day she bounced from Tech Support to Symbay, trying to figure out which issues they were having and how quickly they could be resolved. It was chaotic at best. She no longer felt her efforts were being productive.

When 5:30 rolled around, she couldn't have been happier. It was finally time to de-stress with some Friday-evening yoga.

• • • • •

Lauren had been going to Speakeasy Yoga for about a year and a half. She loved the way it helped clear her mind and mentally reset for the weekend. But today she just couldn't seem to let go. Her mind kept replaying the unpleasant meeting she'd had with Justin. Why couldn't she operate effectively and understand how to improve her role?

When yoga ended, Lauren walked over to a woman she'd recently begun getting to know at the studio.

Claire was older and more experienced than Lauren, but both seemed to have similar personalities. They ambitiously pursued their careers, loved talking to people, and were full of ideas. Claire also happened to be the new Chief Operating Officer (COO) at Max Potential. She was Lauren's boss' boss, overseeing Justin and the whole Account Services department. Yet she was welcoming and kind in a way that put Lauren at ease.

Claire greeted her with a smile. "Hey, how did you like the new instructor today?"

"She was great, but for some reason, I just couldn't let go of the stress from work today."

"Happens to me sometimes, too," responded Claire.

The women continued chatting as they gathered their belongings. On their way out, they took a seat at Speakeasy's Juicing-on-the-patio night.

They relaxed into their seats and continued talking.

"Ever since I've been in Dayton, I keep noticing cute outdoor patios like this," Claire said.

"I can't get enough of them. Dayton's such a charming city." Lauren was eager to get to know Claire better, so she decided to open up the discussion about Claire's history. "How long have you been in Dayton?"

"About three months. I was brought over from my role as Vice President at a tech company in Silicon Valley. Dayton's a change of pace from California. To be honest, I had difficulty adjusting in the first month. How long have you been in Dayton?" Claire asked.

"I've lived here my whole life, but I've only been at Max Potential for five years. I have a daughter in preschool, and we love raising her here."

As the evening went on, Claire wanted to shift the conversation. Picking up on Lauren's comment about not letting go during yoga, she had a feeling it was related to the tension she'd noticed lately at Max Potential. "Did you have something about business on your mind during yoga?" she inquired.

Claire had a calming demeanor. There was something about her that made Lauren feel comfortable speaking honestly. Maybe it was the beautiful evening or maybe it was how Claire had opened up about her difficulty adjusting to Ohio, but Lauren felt comfortable enough to discuss her earlier snafu.

"Okay, big breath. I might as well open up, even though she's a bigwig...here we go," Lauren thought.

"I had a rough day at work," she began. "I work mostly with Symbay, and they've been having technical issues lately using the MaxPT devices. I thought we were handling it, but this morning I received a terrible email from the VP of Operations. The tablets are designed particularly for their industry, but I guess they aren't meeting Symbay's expectations. Then Justin chewed me out for it. It was super stressful, and I'm not sure what to do next."

Claire knew the relationship with Symbay had some issues, but she didn't know the problems went that high up the chain. As the COO, it was her job to know more. "What issues are they having?"

"They feel they aren't getting the value out of the MaxPTs they had originally been promised. And they're experiencing a host of issues that are negatively affecting the user experience. So now we have to run around in crisis mode because the client's threatening to move to another tablet."

"That's a common issue for a lot of companies—too much firefighting. You might put out the fire, but then you don't have any time to find the root causes of a problem to prevent it from happening again," Claire observed.

"Exactly. Firefighting—that's a perfect word for it. I really want to move past this crazy firefighting mode, but I just don't know how to find the help I need. And Justin is so upset, I'm afraid I might not even have a job to worry about."

Claire could tell Lauren sincerely wanted to improve her performance, but she was struggling to determine how. She seemed completely lost in *reactive* problem solving. Her sole focus was solving immediate problems, so she never had the opportunity to *proactively* develop solutions. Furthermore, she was afraid about losing her job. That's not a great place to start.

Claire jumped into coaching mode. "The good news is that what you're experiencing is super common. In fact, the last company I was with dealt with these types of problems all the time."

Lauren breathed a sigh of relief. Claire wasn't judgmental or upset these problems were happening. In fact, she seemed willing to help. "Were you able to solve them?" she asked.

"Absolutely," Claire said confidently. "We used The 5 Disciplines." Claire explained that she'd been working with Max Potential's manufacturing plants in Texas over the last two months. She'd helped them implement the 5 Disciplines to address the hardware problems the MaxPTs have been experiencing, and had already seen improvements. She was now expanding to the service side of Max Potential's operations. And she wanted to start with Lauren.

"What exactly is The 5 Disciplines?" Lauren asked.

"It's a system that helps employees reach their full potential by answering 5 fundamental questions. I've seen it empower employees at every level to improve the way they do their work."

"We start with the first discipline: *Define*. Before you can make improvements to your job, you have to be able to answer this fundamental question: '*What is my job?*'

WHAT IS MY JOB?

"It's absolutely crucial to establish this foundation," Claire explained.

"Okay, sounds simple enough," Lauren reacted.

"Well, you'd think. But it's a bit deeper than you'd guess based on the simplicity of the question.

"To answer it, I'm going to ask you some questions to find the right information. The first one is: *'Who are my customers?'* The customers we serve always define the jobs we perform.

"As an executive, I have a responsibility to the entire organization. I have three main customers: employees, paying customers, and shareholders. And in that order of importance."

Lauren was confused, "How am I your customer, and why am I more important than our customers and the shareholders?"

"If I treat you well, you'll treat our customers well. That generates return for our shareholders. Investing in employees is the smartest investment a company can make... So who are your customers?"

"Hmm. I guess my primary customer is Stan at Symbay," Lauren answered.

"Right, but there's more to it. In The 5 Disciplines, customers are defined in a specific way. Customers are *the people who experience your products or services*. To figure out who your customer is, you have to figure out who receives the *output* of your work."

Claire dug deeper. "Going back to my customers, each group receives a different output from me. Employees receive training, coaching, and fair pay. Customers receive the value-added products that Max Potential creates. Shareholders receive a return on investment."

Lauren stopped her. "I understand I receive fair pay from Max Potential, but where do I receive training and coaching?"

"Because Justin is my direct report, I've just begun providing Justin with training and coaching. When he learns more about his position as a manager, you will receive training and coaching from him."

Surprised, Lauren exclaimed, "That would be great!"

"So back to our previous question, who experiences the output of your work?"

15

"Well, for each new group of users at Symbay, I conduct training sessions. From that perspective, Symbay employees who use the device are my customers.

"I also send invoices to the billing department, so they would be my customers." Lauren thought a bit more. "And I send customization requests to IT when Symbay users want to customize their devices."

"That's excellent. So all of those parties are the recipients of your output. They are the people around whom you should define your job. Makes more sense than simply thinking of your customer as Stan, right?" Claire suggested.

"Absolutely. I know Stan well because I take a lot of technical support calls from his employees."

"Now, as we move forward, remember—there's a reason why *'Who are your customers?'* is the first question in the *Define* step. Everything you do should be focused on serving the customer within your responsibilities."

"A lot of people spend time serving their managers or supervisors. In your situation, it might seem like the person you should be most concerned with is Justin. That's not the case. Having this frame of mind often distracts from the needs of the customer and hurts the company in the long run.

"But let's focus on Symbay for now. If you sent their technical issues to Tech Support every time they called, what else would you have time for? What else could you provide your customer?"

"Geez, that would be tough for me to give up. But I suppose if I didn't resolve technical issues, I'd be able to spend more time talking to my customer. Maybe I'd be able to figure out why they're having problems. And I could figure out why the MaxPTs aren't proving their value."

Claire lit up. Lauren had stumbled upon the key to transforming her role. Claire explained that the things Lauren had just described are the *proactive* aspects of what her role could be. It wasn't just to provide Symbay with working MaxPTs and to manage logistics. It was to proactively deliver solutions to them. This concept is called *the Genius of the And*.[1] "You'll provide the most value by solving problems reactively *AND* proactively," she said.

"I guess you're right. That's a different way of looking at it. I definitely need to think about that more," Lauren responded.

"Good. Over the next week, I want you to think past basic customer requests to understand what else you can provide your clients.

"Before we finish the *Define* step, I want to ask you how well you know the people you work with every day."

"I think I know them pretty well. I've been in the department for six months, so...yeah, I feel pretty comfortable," Lauren answered off the cuff.

Claire smiled. "So then you know how many pets Justin has?"

Lauren almost began to laugh. "How many pets? Well, no. Is that really relevant to my job?"

"Absolutely. Have you heard of the Yogi Berra quote, 'Baseball is 90% mental and the other half is physical'?"

Lauren laughed. "No, I don't think I've heard that one. It's very confusing."

"You're right," Claire said with a smile. "It's ludicrous, but what it's getting at is that the mental aspect of baseball is much more important than the physical aspect. In The 5 Disciplines, the quote can be rewritten as 'An organization is 90% people and the other half is process.'"

"Okay, I'm starting to understand. Basically, people are more important to a business's success than we normally think," Lauren postulated.

"Exactly, and that's a central theme in The 5 Disciplines. People in this method of thinking represent the *art* of business, while process represents the *science*. Both have to work in tandem

---

[1] Jim Collins and Jerry Porras, *Built to Last*, (New York: HarperBusiness, 3rd Edition, 1994)

so they are interwoven into each step of The 5 Disciplines, but nothing is more important than people."

"Well if that's the question, then no, I don't know Justin from a personal perspective at all."

"Over the next week, I'm challenging you to get to know him on a personal level. If you can tell me if he's in a relationship, what hobbies he has, and what his pet's names are, you'll be making real progress."

"Okay. I'll invite him to coffee and see if it works."

"Perfect!" Claire exclaimed. "The last thing I want to discuss is the purpose of your job."

"My purpose? That's quite a lofty question…" Lauren mused.

"Your purpose statement is essentially a summary of your job. What is the purpose of your work? Because your purpose statement is so central to our progress moving forward, I'd like you to think about this one and tell me next Friday."

Lauren perked her head up, "Next Friday?"

"Yes." Claire grinned. When Claire first learned The 5 Disciplines, she'd had a great mentor, which had made all the difference in the world. Now she wanted to provide the same coaching to Lauren. "Based on what you've told me; I'd like to keep meeting to talk about The 5 Disciplines. You have some work to do next week," Claire smiled. "But I think another Yoga and Juicing night next Friday would be a perfect time to talk about step 2—*Measure*."

"That would be fantastic. So does that mean we've come to the end of our lesson for today?"

Claire smiled. "Yes, I think I've given you more than enough to think about."

"I agree," Lauren said as she finished her last sip of juice.

Claire quickly sent a text to her assistant to set a meeting with Justin. Claire wanted to let Justin know she had begun to mentor Lauren.

The two women spoke about their plans for the weekend while they gathered their things to leave. As Lauren walked to her car, she had a strange feeling of excitement. She couldn't believe Claire was so willing to help her. In only a short time, Claire had begun to clarify why she was experiencing problems with Symbay and Justin.

With a feeling of excitement, she hopped into her car and drove home. She knew the road ahead would require a course correction, and would be a challenge, but even this faint feeling of empowerment made her anxious to explore The 5 Disciplines further.

• • • • •

On Monday morning, Lauren was ready to hit the ground running. After she put down her things and grabbed a cup of coffee, she began to plan out her day.

"Okay. Claire gave me a lot to think about and get done this week. But first I need to take care of my main customer. So what does Symbay need right at this moment?"

Lauren,

I have heard numerous times over the last three months that our employees are having difficulty using the MaxPTs. We are experiencing technical issues and aren't able to seamlessly integrate the tablets into our daily operations. We can't afford to continue having issues while seeing no real, long-term solutions. The tablets are not showing the long-term value we hoped for. As a company, it may be time for us to explore other options.

Please respond with how you plan to fix this problem.

— Phillip

Lauren thought about what had led to the email she received on Friday. "Right! We've got to let them know we are working as hard as possible to fix their technical issues."

She read through the email from Phillip, Symbay's VP of Operations, one more time.

"Long-term value? Is that really my role? All I've been doing is focusing on technical issues, but clearly that isn't working for him," she thought.

She drafted an email in response, expressing her sincere regret for the difficulties Symbay had experienced and her desire to repair the relationship moving forward.

Lauren would work with Tech Support to handle Symbay's immediate issues. She would ensure that every existing complaint was resolved as quickly as possible. When she was finished, she emailed Stan to make sure he knew that Tech Support had a plan to solve the technical issues.

When she had the most pressing issues buttoned up, she sat down at her desk to dive into answering the fundamental question of the *Define* step, "*What is my job?*"

"Well, Claire said I need to get to know the people I work with better. Ugh, that means sitting down to talk with Justin," she thought to herself. She began drafting a meeting invite to Justin, despite her desire to avoid having another unpleasant conversation with him.

She sent the email to Justin. The location wasn't at work like usual; it was at the coffee shop down the street where people from her office often met.

To her surprise, Justin accepted the invite without sending a meeting agenda or an argument about which day would be best. Maybe this meeting wouldn't be too bad.

With that settled, Lauren began to consider the proactive aspects of her role. When she had resolved the immediate technical issues, what else could she provide her customers?

"What did Claire say again? Oh yeah—*the genius of the and.*" Suddenly it struck Lauren. "Phillip wants me to show the value in the MaxPTs. To do that, I need to see the bigger picture of what Symbay needs, almost like a consultant." Lauren was excited. She'd had an "a-ha!" moment and couldn't wait to tell Claire.

"I bet that's what my purpose statement should be about!"

Lauren tried to define her purpose statement while considering all aspects of her role. She wrote down several iterations, trying to include the details of what she did. The statement kept ending up too complicated.

After an hour of examining her work and exploring what she provided customers, Lauren considered the idea of thinking proactively.

"I need to figure out how the MaxPTs can be valuable to Symbay!" She hurriedly scribbled down what would become her final purpose statement.

"My purpose statement is as follows: *I provide training and consulting that optimizes the MaxPTs value to Symbay's business.*"

Lauren's phone began to ring. It was her main point of contact at Symbay, Stan.

"Hello?" Lauren answered hesitantly.

"Hi, Lauren. I wanted to give you a quick ring for two reasons."

Lauren held her breath. Would the next part be good or bad?

"First, I wanted to compliment you on how you handled the issue we had late last week. Phillip can be pretty intense, but you've done a great job of resolving our issues and letting us know you are dedicated to getting us back on track."

Lauren relaxed a bit in her seat. "It's great to hear you say that. We are doing everything we can to address Phillip's concerns."

"I also wanted to discuss scheduling a training session for some of the new MaxPT users on our team. In the last month, we've brought a new department on board to begin using the devices."

"Yes, your purchasing department, right? I'm looking forward to bringing them onboard." She suspected it was this influx of new users that brought Phillip's attention to the MaxPTs and made him wonder if investing further into the product was a good idea.

"That can certainly be arranged. I'll reach out with times to schedule a training session, and I'll personally attend."

"Perfect! Well then, I'll look for your email and respond with a date that works. Other than that, I'll be in touch if any other issues come up."

Lauren said goodbye and hung up. She was glad Stan seemed to be developing a more positive attitude towards the situation, but she knew she was still in hot water with Phillip.

For the rest of the day, Lauren prepared for the training session with Symbay and examined her job in the way Claire had suggested. She articulated to herself exactly what she thought her role needed to be, and just as importantly, what wasn't part of her job. Her thinking began to transform as she thought about her role according to the guidelines of the *Define* step. By the end of the day, she was excited to show Claire what she had come up with.

$$\bullet \quad \bullet \quad \bullet \quad \bullet \quad \bullet$$

The next morning, Lauren and Justin met at the coffee shop. Justin sat down in his typical rigid fashion. Lauren calmly sipped her coffee.

"So, how long have you worked at Max Potential?"

"It'll be eleven years in January," he responded, curious about why Lauren wanted to have coffee with him. Since Claire had been coaching him to be more social, he reluctantly accepted the invite and was going to do his best at being "social"—whatever that meant.

"That's longer than I thought. Have you enjoyed it?" Lauren asked.

Justin thought about Lauren's question. He didn't normally ask himself if he enjoyed his day-to-day. "I suppose I have. It's a lot more relaxed than what I was doing before."

"Relaxed?" Lauren thought to herself. If this was Justin relaxed, she'd hate to see him wound up. "What do you mean?" she asked.

"Well, before I worked in the private sector, I was a colonel in the military. Growing up, my dad was also in the military, so I'm used to a rigid discipline structure. Max Potential is much more informal. I've been enjoying that aspect of the job."

"Interesting. I had no idea you were in the military. Do you miss it?" Lauren asked.

"From time to time. But I go running with my military friend Doug every morning, so I still get the same exercise and structure I had 15 years ago."

"Oh, that's awesome. I'm a runner too. I don't go every morning, though," Lauren noted with a smile.

The two continued their casual conversation. Lauren began to understand why Justin operated in such a rigid fashion and was figuring out how to open a dialogue with him. By the time they finished their coffee, she felt better prepared to work with Justin to resolve the problems they were having with Symbay.

"I guess time will tell," she thought to herself as they headed back to the office.

DEFINE STEP SUMMARY

The following questions can be asked in the *Define* step to gather information that answers the question *"What is my job?"*

Who are my customers and what do I provide them?

Your job is defined by what you produce to internal or external customers. Customers are the people who experience your products and/or services. The quality and timeliness of your products/services is what you provide them.

- Lauren's main customers are Symbay employees who use the MaxPTs. Her other customers can be divided into internal and external customers. Internally, she provides outputs for the billing department and IT. Her boss is not her customer because the output of her work is not intended for him.

What are my work processes?

Work processes are the activities you do every day that produce the products and/or services you provide your customers. As an example, scheduling and delivering training are work processes for Lauren.

- Lauren's work processes had never been articulated because her role was new within Max Potential.

Who are my suppliers and what do they provide me?

Suppliers are the people that provide information or materials to help you do your work processes.

- Justin provides Lauren with training and coaching to help her develop her strategic thinking skills.

How well do I know the people I work with every day?

In every organization, almost all work requires the ability to work with others to accomplish the overall task of delivering products and/or services to customers. To work effectively with others, it is necessary to have a good working relationship with each person. Doing so requires knowing them on a personal level.

- Lauren knew the people she worked with in her old job in Tech Support. In her new role she did not know her boss, Justin, as well as her contacts at Symbay.

What is my purpose?

A purpose statement is a simple job description that may include the customers you serve or the products and/or services you produce.

- Lauren's purpose statement is: *I provide training and consulting that optimizes the MaxPTs value to Symbay's business.*

2

MEASURE

Am I Doing a Good Job?

STEP 2 MEASURE

It was finally Friday again. The week had been tiresome, but productive. Lauren was ready for yoga.

To prepare for what she hoped would be another enlightening conversation with Claire, she wrote down a summary of her insights from the *Define* step.

That night at Speakeasy Yoga, she was excited for class to end. She rushed over to Claire to explain the progress she'd made defining her role.

"Yoga and Juicing night again?" Lauren asked.

"Absolutely!" Claire exclaimed.

The two women sat down at the same table they'd enjoyed the Friday before.

"Tell me, what did you learn about Justin?"

"I learned a lot about him this week. We even went out for coffee," Lauren told Claire.

"That was a smart idea. Any good department is fueled by trust between team members, and you can't build trust until you've established a personal relationship. What do you know about Justin now that you didn't before?"

"Well, at the beginning of his professional career, he didn't work in Accounts. In fact, he wasn't in the private sector at all. For years, he was in the military, which explains why he expects me to be so structured," Lauren divulged. "It seems like he wants to grow the department, but I think he feels most comfortable creating his own processes for his direct reports to follow."

"I'm glad you took the time to get to know him on a personal level. As we continue through The 5 Disciplines, keep thinking about those relationships. And don't restrict them to just Justin. Build rapport with the client and other people you interact with. That's the kind of information that creates relationships which allow you to perform at your highest level. Without those relationships, it doesn't matter how technically proficient you are or how hard you work—you'll hit a ceiling and be restricted.

Relationships are what make companies great and what make employees great within those companies."

"I'm getting off my soapbox now" Claire smiled. "How about the nuts and bolts of your role? Did you nail down who your customer is and what you provide to them?" Claire asked.

Lauren responded and explained the clarity she'd achieved over the past week. Claire was impressed by her progress. She could tell Lauren was sincerely committed to becoming empowered within her role. She could also see Lauren now understood she wasn't just an order taker. Lauren needed to be a consultant to Symbay to deliver the value Phillip was looking for.

After Lauren told Claire her purpose statement, she had a thought. "Now that I've determined my purpose statement, do you mind if I ask what yours is?"

"It's funny you should ask. I have it written above my desk so I see it every day. My purpose statement is: *I help create an environment where success happens for employees, customers, and shareholders.* It's simple and centered around my customers."

Claire was inspired to push Lauren to the next step: *Measure.*

"It seems like you've done a great job *Defining* your role. The next step is figuring out how to *Measure* what you do. In other words, *"Am I doing a good job?"*

AM I DOING A GOOD JOB?

"That makes sense. If I had a way to measure what I do, then at least I could prove to Justin that things aren't all doom and gloom, like he makes them seem sometimes." Lauren liked the idea.

"Exactly. And you'd know where you stand and what future achievement could look like. Just as there was an art and a science to defining your role, there's also an art and science to measuring your role," Claire elaborated.

"That makes sense. But how would I measure my relationships with my coworkers and my boss? That seems like a super vague thing to measure," Lauren challenged.

"This is actually a focal point of the improvement system we're discussing. The key metric of good working relationships is *trust*, and you have to be able to measure it. That's why I first want to ask you what the trust equation is with the people you work with."

Lauren was confused. "Trust equation? That sounds odd. How on Earth can you measure trust?"

Claire was happy Lauren was asking the right types of questions. "It's actually pretty simple. Despite the complexity of human relationships, there's a simple formula you can use." Claire pulled a napkin from the dispenser on the table. She scribbled down an equation and passed the napkin to Lauren.

Trust = number of promises kept divided by number of promises made

Claire went further. "So according to this, how would you build trust with Justin?" she asked.

"Well, according to this equation, I keep my promises. I show up to work on time. I meet deadlines. I make sure when I say I'll do something; I actually do it. If I'm unable to meet a deadline, I explain why."

"Yes. And the other half of the trust equation is listening and building rapport through *open and honest communication*," Claire elaborated.

Lauren liked the way that sounded. If she could be honest with Justin, things would be much different. "Wow, that would be a shift. I often feel like I have to keep my mouth shut or solve problems quickly before Justin gets on my case. We really haven't established open and honest communication at all."

"It's a difficult thing to do. Especially when there's tension. But learning the personal details of the people you work with will encourage open and honest communication. Include keeping your promises on a consistent basis, and you've got the ingredients to build trust-based relationships."

"So I need to understand what my trust equation is with the people I work with and then I can begin to measure my relationships at work?" Lauren questioned.

"Yes. Look at Max Potential's relationship with Symbay. The sales team probably promised a product that would help their business, but now they're seeing issues that waste time and money," Claire explained.

"So there was a lack of open and honest communication, but there was also a measurable difference between promises made and promises kept," Lauren explored.

"You've got it. It's a mix of both. Trust is the foundation of all successful business relationships," Claire concluded.

"You also have to be able to measure your success. When you leave work every day, do you know what has made you successful or unsuccessful that day?" Claire asked.

"I kind of judge it based on how smoothly the day went, but now that I think about it, no, I really don't know what Justin is going to use to gauge my performance. Geez, you'd think that would be something I'd know." She started getting annoyed thinking about how in the dark Justin had kept her. "When I was in Tech Support, it was pretty easy. Did you answer every call? Did you resolve the issues quickly?"

"That's typical with a job like yours that's gotten more complex. However, it's really important to understand how you're performing and why you're doing well or could be doing better. Like *Define*, you need to put everything in terms of the customer. So, *what are your customers' expectations?*"

"Hmm, well Stan seems like he really just wants to know that the MaxPTs are working correctly, and when they aren't, that we're solving the problem quickly."

"That's good. Many customer expectations are centered on timeliness of service and quality of product. In order to build trust with the client, you need to consistently deliver both. It seems Phillip is seeing a lack of quality.

"In addition, he's also mentioned larger concerns where his expectations aren't being met. If you think about what someone on the leadership team would care about, what does that look like?" Claire asked.

"Phillip said he expects the MaxPTs to deliver value. I don't exactly know what that means," Lauren explored.

"It seems like you've spent plenty of time listening to the client to solve problems, but could spend more time probing beneath the surface. If you aren't sure how the MaxPTs can deliver the value Phillip is looking for, then you need to find out," Claire answered. "As we discovered last week, being proactive in your role means thinking of yourself as a consultant. Consultants have to understand the customer's deeper issues if they are going to provide additional value."

Lauren was starting to understand how her role needed to shift. "Then it sounds like I need to learn more about Phillip."

"Or at the very least, more about Symbay's business," Claire suggested. "When you know what your customers' expectations are, you need to measure how fully you're meeting those expectations."

Lauren was confused. "Measure them? It's not like measuring a cup of sugar."

"Not exactly. With the expectations you've created, they anticipate a certain turnaround time when they have a technical issue. And Phillip has made it clear he expects a minimal number of service complaints. If you collect any data or information that relates to your customer's expectations, you can know how consistently you're meeting those expectations," Claire noted. "But you'll have to do your own research to figure out exactly what those metrics should be."

"Well, I know Tech Support collects all service call information, but I've never seen anything that shows it. I could also do some digging around in our department. What should I be looking for?"

"Well, this information can come in many forms. For example, you could gather information by observing and recording what you see. Or it could be measurable data. A lot of companies now are equipped to provide a wealth of customer information. It could even be a survey that you create. It's all about figuring out how to use the data based on what will be most helpful.

"If you don't have the information you need, you have to get it. This is where you begin to move from *reactive* to *proactive*. Now that you're in the *Measure* step, you'll identify what the ideal metrics for success are based on your customer. Then you'll have every bit of information you need to go out and get the data to measure it yourself."

Lauren perked up. She liked the idea that if she wasn't getting what she needed, she had the tools to solve those problems herself. "Proactive, right? I used to work in Tech Support. I'll work with them on Monday to see what I can find."

"Cheers to that," Claire said as she raised her glass.

The women clinked glasses and sipped their juice.

"In addition to measuring your customers' expectations, you need to measure your success against the larger goals of your department. You should always know how your day-to-day activities contribute to those goals. What does success look like for your department and are you contributing to that success?" Claire asked.

"I have no idea what the goals of our department are. I'm guessing I'll have to meet with Justin to answer this one," Lauren said.

"Absolutely. It's that combination of customer expectations and departmental goals that will make up your metrics for success, which takes a bit of work to nail down. I can, however, make your job a little easier. I have a metric I use for myself that I've also used for the last three months to help the Texas plant build their metrics. And in the next couple of months, I want it to be one every department uses," Claire said.

"Every department? That seems like a big goal," Lauren responded with skepticism.

"Yep, every one. And that's because it's central to the whole system. The most important metric for me and every Max Potential employee is *the number of implemented improvements per employee per year*."

"I'm not sure what that means."

"Every time you implement an improvement, there's something you can track. In fact, implementing individual improvements is the foundation of The 5 Disciplines. There's a reason it's about implemented improvements and not the number of ideas or suggestions."

"To implement an improvement, you have to be disciplined, but people aren't born with self-discipline. They learn it. That's what self-leadership is all about—learning to be disciplined and to continuously improve. The 5 Disciplines gives you the tools to do that."

"I really like this self-leadership idea," Lauren responded, beaming at the idea of taking control of her career.

"I do, too. That's what pulled me into The 5 Disciplines in the first place. Ever since, I've maintained the same system of thought to always maximize my potential at work," Claire expounded.

"Well, it looks like I have quite a bit of work to do this week, but I can't wait. I know this isn't typical Friday evening conversation," Lauren smiled, "but I'm so glad we're doing this."

Claire agreed.

As they finished their juice, Lauren's mind stirred over the information she'd just learned. The next week would be a heavy week of data-gathering. And then she had the training session with Symbay, but she could tell she was headed towards a new and exciting direction in her career.

• • • • •

Lauren's first concern when the week began was getting everything squared away for the training session with Stan. "Customer first," she thought. Claire's coaching had already started to work.

Lauren scheduled the training session with a couple of emails and then proceeded to review the existing training materials. They'd been standardized across every account, so she was only responsible for teaching the manual to new users. She got so bored at these training sessions.

"Part of the job," she shrugged.

As she re-evaluated the manual from a different perspective, she let her mind wander. "When I train the new users, what do they expect?

"Well, since they're new to the devices, they'll expect to have a thorough grasp of how to use them. I could measure that!"

She began drafting questions to ask the trainees. It would be a survey to see how effective she'd been in training them. She could also ask additional information like how they planned to use the devices and what they thought of the training. She could compare the surveys over time as more Symbay employees went through the training.

With the training session scheduled for Thursday, she decided she needed to review her survey with Justin sooner rather than later. She also needed to ask him about the department's metrics.

Lauren remembered Claire's advice about building open and honest communication. She picked up the phone and called Justin's office phone instead of sending him an email.

"Hey, Justin!"

"Lauren, how can I help you?" he asked, sounding just as rigid and stern as ever.

But Lauren kept an upbeat tone. "I had a quick question for you. Before I meet with Stan and his team, it would be great to sit down and discuss how we can gauge the training session. I'd also like to discuss how we can approach fixing the problems we've been experiencing with Symbay."

Justin was impressed. Lauren had started to think proactively about her relationship with Symbay. "That would be great," Justin replied. Lauren was pleased she'd gotten him to lighten up a bit.

"Ha! You'll warm up to me eventually," she thought. She of course didn't say this to Justin. Instead, she quickly wrapped up the call.

Now it was time to get some data.

To prepare for the meeting with Justin, she went to Tech Support to gather data that would help her establish metrics and evaluate her performance.

When she opened the door, she saw the familiar faces she used to see every day. She reminisced when she walked into the room. After briefly greeting her former colleagues, she walked over to her previous supervisor, Garrett. Lauren knew that he meticulously gathered data from all customer interactions with Tech Support. Lauren knew he was the one to talk to about gathering the information she was looking for.

Garrett stood up from his desk to say hello. "Lauren! Fancy seeing you here. What brings you to Tech Support?"

"Hey, Garret! Good to see you. I'm actually here to gather some data. I know Tech Support keeps comprehensive records of customer service calls, and I'm wondering if you can help me pull Symbay's data," Lauren explained.

"Sure, not a problem. What kind of data are you looking for?"

"I'm not quite sure. I'm trying to develop a picture of how well we're meeting Symbay's expectations. It would help to get a deeper look at their call data," Lauren responded. "Do you have that information?"

"Yes, we do. Since the account opened last year, we've gathered a ton of data—how many service calls made, what they're about, how long it takes us to resolve the issues. The list goes on and on. It's really about how you want to use the data," Garret said. "Let me show you how to view the numbers. It can be as simple or complex as you want it to be." Garrett gestured for Lauren to follow him. As they looked through the data, Lauren could already start to see patterns. Service calls in general had been on the rise. She had no idea, however, how many service calls Max Potential had received from Symbay lately.

Lauren said goodbye and walked back to her desk. Around mid-afternoon she received an email with the data Garrett had promised. He was right when he said there was a lot of data. After an hour of combing through graphs and feedback, it became clear Lauren would need some help. She decided to pull out interesting metrics and bring the data to her meeting with Justin.

· · · · ·

The next day, she was all set for her meeting with Justin. She'd gathered the data and prepared an agenda. "Look at me...on my game. I can do this," she thought as she knocked on his door.

She entered his office. "Hi Justin." He sat facing straight towards the door in his typical military fashion, but he greeted her with a warmer welcome than she expected. Maybe developing a personal understanding with each other was starting to pay off.

"Hi, Lauren. What did you want to talk about?"

"After we received the email from Phillip, I started thinking about metrics for success and how I can continuously make improvements to the business relationship with Symbay in the future."

Justin sat back in his seat. "I'm happy to hear you say that, and I'd like to see you move forward with that idea."

She breathed a sigh of relief. "Off to a good start." She'd started to realize if she could speak in Justin's systematic, data-driven way, he'd be much more willing to hear her out.

"Because this is a relatively new position, clear-cut success metrics have not yet been created, and I'm having difficulty determining if I'm succeeding. I'd like to brainstorm some ways to measure that. I think it would be helpful to start by understanding the department's metrics for success."

"Actually, that's just what our leadership team has been discussing lately. From my perspective, I'm concerned with efficiency and device effectiveness. The department needs to set up the devices and monitor them in such a way that we minimize technical issues. If we can do that, we can minimize our risk of losing big accounts like Symbay," he explained.

"That makes perfect sense. I've actually pulled some data from Tech Support to measure how we're doing."

Justin perked up. Now Lauren was speaking his language.

"Based on what you've said, I think it would be great to look at how many service calls we're receiving per week," Lauren responded.

"I agree. If we can minimize that number, we'd be moving in the right direction," Justin said. But then he introduced a metric Lauren didn't feel as great about. "We also need to minimize the amount of time the Account Coordinators are speaking with the client. In your role, time spent in conversation takes away from the rest of your responsibilities."

"Okay, open and honest communication, Lauren," she coached herself. "If you don't agree with something, you need to be transparent about why."

She decided to challenge his point. "I can see how we would want to aim for efficiency. As long as time is spent wisely, though, I actually see a benefit to speaking with the client. For instance, with the training session I have with Symbay later this week, if I invest time with the client upfront, I can make sure they use the devices in a way that prevents technical issues in the future."

Justin was skeptical, but Lauren continued before he could disagree.

"In fact, I've developed a survey for the training session that will measure the effectiveness of the training. We can then compare that with measurements of service calls for those trainees."

Justin was willing to give it a try. Lauren was taking control of the situation and was prepared with data to back her up. "If you show me you can lower service calls per week, I'd be willing to discuss you spending more time talking with the client."

"Great. I appreciate that," Lauren said.

Justin thought of something else. "We also want to resolve issues in no more than 24 hours. We believe this consistency will help us grow accounts in the future."

"Agreed. I will monitor that data as well. I'd also like to measure our progress towards overcoming Phillip's concern that the MaxPTs are not providing value. To do that, I'd like to send a survey questionnaire to the Symbay parties responsible for managing the MaxPTs. With that information, we'll get a better understanding of their perspective."

"I can agree with that. I'd like to monitor those communications," Justin said.

"Absolutely." Lauren concluded the meeting feeling that she had concrete ways to show Justin how she was performing. She'd also have a better understanding of Symbay's experience with the MaxPTs. Things were beginning to take shape in the way Claire had described. Lauren couldn't wait for the next step.

• • • • •

Lauren rang the bell to enter the Symbay building. She was a bit nervous. With all of the customer complaints and the hot water she found herself in, she didn't want to mess up.

The receptionist buzzed her in. Stan stood at the desk. She liked working with Stan. He was easy to get along with, cheerful, and seemed like he wanted what was best for everyone. Lauren was glad Phillip wasn't there. She was already nervous enough.

Stan greeted her and showed her where to set up. Lauren began laying out the training manuals. It seemed a bit antiquated to be training users about a digital device using physical training manuals. "Oh well," she thought. "That's the way I was taught to do it."

As she finished setting up, people began to filter in. When everyone had settled, she began.

"Thank you for coming. Today we're going to set up your devices and train you on their day-to-day operation."

Lauren launched into the manual. As she took the group through it, she noticed a lot of the content wasn't relevant to Symbay. Walking through so much information at one time diluted the relevant material.

The meeting took two hours, but Lauren felt it hadn't been the most worthwhile time spent. At the end, she asked the group to fill out the survey.

If nothing else, at least she had her first data point to begin measuring the training.

• • • • •

The week went by and it was Friday again. Lauren had completed the *Measure* step and had firm measurements to evaluate her performance. She was excited to tell Claire about her progress. Unfortunately, Claire sent an email letting Lauren know she couldn't make it to yoga.

Hi Lauren,

I had a late meeting pop up and won't be able to make it to yoga tonight. Because we won't be able to discuss The 5 Disciplines this week, I'll be sending you an email on Monday to get you started on the next step: *Analyze*.

I can't wait to hear of your progress during our next conversation.

Thanks,

Claire

Lauren was disappointed, but at least her progress on The 5 Disciplines wouldn't be stalled. She looked forward to the next step.

Before she packed up to head to yoga, she received a call. It was from one of the trainees she'd coached the day before.

"Hi Lauren. Getting set up on the MaxPT, and I keep getting locked out of the device. You were so helpful at our training session, I figured I'd just give you a quick ring."

This exact problem happened often. She knew a quick workaround and could fix the issue in a couple of minutes, but remembering Justin's desire for her to forward these requests to Tech Support, she responded differently than normal. "I'm glad you reached out. This is a pretty common issue. I'm going to forward your call to our Tech Support team, who are the most qualified people to solve this problem for you. Tech Support will also be your point of contact for technical issues in the future."

Lauren forwarded the call to Tech Support. She was proud of herself. Because she knew her role, she could forego tasks that weren't hers and stay on top of her core responsibilities.

As she walked out the door to her car, she had a thought.

"I'm supposed to be proactive. If I'm not supposed to handle this issue, what should I be doing?" Then she had a moment of insight. "I need to figure out why this issue keeps happening and fix it for Symbay."

With that, Lauren knew exactly what she would be doing next week—*analyzing*.

MEASURE STEP SUMMARY

The following questions can be asked in *Measure* step to answer the question "*Am I doing a good job?*"

How do I measure trust?

This can be done using the trust equation (number of promises delivered divided by the number of promises made) plus open and honest communication.

- Lauren knew the promises of increased productivity for Symbay were not being fulfilled. She also knew she didn't have a trust-based relationship with Justin or Symbay.

What are my customers' expectations?

Most customer expectations are directly related to the quality (defect-free) and timeliness of your products and services.

- The MaxPTs were delivered on time, but some of them were defective. Lauren did not fully understand how the MaxPT was supposed to help improve Symbay's business, which was their primary expectation.

How do I measure my customers' expectations?

Measuring means collecting data or numbers that link directly to your customers' expectations. This data can be as simple or as detailed as needed. It can take the form of any information that provides a clear and concrete picture of customer expectations.

- Lauren knew Tech Support was measuring the number of service calls from Symbay, the duration of each call, and the percentage of complaints solved within

24 hours. She had not seen any graphs showing trends over time or the type of problems related to the calls. Lauren had no idea how to measure if the MaxPTs were helping to improve Symbay's business.

Am I aligned to my department's metrics?

Ideally, each person should have two to three metrics that align directly with their department's metrics.

- Lauren was aligned with the metric of the number of service calls. The Service Department did not have any metrics for Account Managers that would tell her if she was doing a good job. Since Lauren was also responsible for training, she adopted the training survey score as a key metric. Finally, Claire said the most important metric for her and every employee of Symbay is the number of improvements implemented per year.

How do I implement my metrics?

An important aspect of implementing metrics is determining measurement frequency.

- Lauren's metrics were:

  1. service calls per week;

  2. training scores after each training session (scale from one to five); and

  3. number of implemented improvements per month. Each metric could be shown in a line graph over time.

3

ANALYZE

How Do
I Analyze
My Job?

STEP 3 ANALYZE

The first thing Lauren noticed on Monday morning was an email from Claire.

Lauren,

Welcome to the third step of The 5 Disciplines—*Analyze*. This week we'll answer the fundamental question *"How do I analyze my job?"*

HOW DO I ANALYZE MY JOB?

First, I'd like you to focus on your coaching and training needs. You'll need to analyze your strengths and weaknesses to learn where you need to improve. Getting feedback from others will provide useful information. Sometimes, it can be intimidating to ask your boss to describe your strengths and weaknesses. I suggest you start by asking a colleague you admire who feels comfortable being honest with you.

Then we're going to dive into your role to determine what's creating the firefighting and customer dissatisfaction you've been experiencing. More on this to come.

Looking forward to hearing about your progress!

Claire

"Strengths and weaknesses. Hmm," Lauren pondered the question. As she was thinking, she received a call.

Yet again, it was a Symbay employee calling her with a complaint. As the caller described the issue, she knew exactly what to do. From working in Tech Support, she knew the MaxPTs like the back of her hand. As before, she simply forwarded the call to Tech Support. She knew she could answer the question, but also knew it wasn't her job. She suddenly remembered her mother telling her, "For everything you say 'yes' to, you are saying 'no' to something else." She needed to commit her efforts to proactive work right now.

When she hung up, she realized one of her strengths was a strong technical knowledge of the product. She knew how to help people use them effectively, she knew how to avoid technical issues, and she knew how to modify the device to achieve certain functions.

"Well, there we go. That's a strength," she said under her breath.

As she did, Gene, one of the other Account Coordinators, walked past her desk and heard her.

"Did you say something?" he asked.

Lauren laughed. "Oh no! Just talking to myself."

She respected Gene's opinion. He'd been working as an Account Coordinator at Max Potential for six months longer than Lauren and always seemed to handle his accounts without difficulty. He hadn't been with Max Potential as long as Lauren, but he worked as an Account Coordinator for another company before switching jobs. If anyone knew what it took to be a great Account Coordinator, it would be Gene.

"Hey, since you stopped by, would you be available for lunch today?"

"Yeah, that would be great," Gene responded.

Lauren went back to work. In addition to her typical Monday morning tasks, she typed an email asking Stan to respond with some basic feedback on the MaxPTs. The more information she could gather to analyze what needed to be improved, the better.

By the time lunch rolled around, Lauren was starving. She met with Gene at Ty's Burger Barn, one of her favorite local restaurants, and quickly ordered her food so she could get down to business.

"Thanks for inviting me to lunch," Gene said. "What did you want to talk about?"

"Over the past few weeks, I've been working with a mentor to improve my work. I'm not sure if you heard, but we received an email from Symbay's VP a couple weeks ago letting us know he was considering dropping the MaxPTs and may be looking for an alternative device."

"Yikes. That's a big account. I bet Justin didn't take that well," Gene responded.

"Not at all. He got upset, and I knew things needed to change. So now I'm working through a system called The 5 Disciplines. At the moment, I'm trying to determine my strengths and weaknesses so I can understand my coaching and training needs. With your experience, I wanted to ask for feedback and learn how you trained to become an Account Coordinator," Lauren expounded.

"The 5 Disciplines, I'll have to look that up. But in terms of feedback...hmm..." Gene paused. He thought for a moment. "From what I've seen, you know more about the MaxPTs than all of the Account Coordinators, so that's a big asset. I guess sometimes you lean on that knowledge instead of venturing out of your comfort zone.

"In my opinion, the most important aspect of this role is being able to think strategically for the customer. Instead of telling my customers how to use the MaxPTs, the first thing I do is ask them what their needs are. I learn about their business and then work with them to customize the devices based on how I think the MaxPTs can help. From my perspective and the times that we've worked together, you might consider thinking more strategically on behalf of your customer," Gene continued.

"Also, you have great people skills. They wouldn't have promoted you to this position if you didn't. That'll be a great asset as you learn your customer's business."

Lauren was glad to hear Gene's perspective.

"I do love working with the customer. Has Justin helped train you in the past?" she asked.

Gene responded, "Justin can be a bit difficult to work with. He won't go out of his way, but when I've asked him for help, he's been an excellent coach."

"I'm really glad to hear that," Lauren said with relief.

Hearing that Justin could provide useful training and coaching opened a path to improving her weaknesses as well as building her strengths.

Lauren and Gene finished their meals with casual conversation. She always enjoyed Gene's company and was happy she'd invited him to lunch. Claire's advice was right again. Building relationships had helped her move closer to feeling empowered as an Account Coordinator.

When she returned to her desk, she immediately sent an email to Claire.

To her surprise, Claire responded within the hour, but not with an email. Lauren received a meeting invite for the next day with a brief description attached.

"Lauren,

The next questions get pretty in-depth, so before we meet tomorrow, we'll need some data. Please contact Stan to find out his most critical issues with the MaxPTs, how he's feeling since Phillip sent that first email, and what his general feedback is based on his contact with you over the past six months. You'll also need to schedule another meeting with Justin after ours. Looking forward to diving in deeper!"

That afternoon, she called Stan as Claire had instructed.

"Hi, Stan. Is now a good time to talk?"

"It is. How can I help?" Stan responded. Lauren openly explained she had been thoroughly evaluating the MaxPTs. Phillip's email caused her to analyze the situation to find ways to make improvements. "With that in mind, what is the biggest challenge when using the MaxPT?"

"I'm happy to hear you're investing so much effort into our account. Personally, the MaxPTs have helped make my life a lot easier, so if we can figure out a way to prove that value to Phillip, I think we'll be in a really good place.

"In response to your question, right now the most important issue is making sure we stop experiencing technical issues. It's causing agitation and we aren't getting as much out of the MaxPTs as we had hoped. Our users aren't sure how to use the devices fully, and the devices aren't functioning in the way we need."

Lauren could tell the relationship with Symbay still needed some serious repair work. "I'm grateful you've taken the time to explain that to me," she began. "We are experiencing growth, but I can assure you we are improving our processes to accommodate that growth. My full attention is on understanding why Symbay is experiencing technical issues and resolving those issues as quickly as possible."

"I'm glad to hear you say that. I'm willing to do whatever I can to help," Stan responded.

Lauren remembered Claire's advice to focus on the people side of improvement. If she wanted to become empowered in her role, she needed to build and strengthen as many professional relationships as possible. Her relationship with Stan was another great opportunity.

"One thing that might be helpful for both of us is to set up bi-weekly check-ins like this. That'll help ensure that things are moving in the right direction. It will also make it easier for you to report our progress to your leadership team. Would that work for you?" she asked.

"Absolutely. That would be helpful." Stan's tone was already sounding friendlier.

Lauren agreed to send a recurring invite. She thanked Stan for his time and ended the conversation.

Now she had all the data she needed to talk with Claire and learn the rest of the Analyze step.

• • • • •

It was Tuesday morning at 9:55, five minutes before her meeting with Claire. Lauren looked back and forth from her screen to her clock in anticipation.

"This'll be our first actual meeting at work. I think I'm a little nervous," she thought to herself.

The clocked ticked to 9:58. "Oh, I can be two minutes early. I'm not waiting any longer." She sprung out of her chair and quickly walked to the conference room.

When Claire walked into the room, Lauren was struck by how sharply her presence commanded attention compared to her casual demeanor at yoga. Lauren sat up a bit straighter, ready to dive into the conversation.

"Thank you for meeting with me!" Claire said. "The questions we'll go over today are more complex and will directly set up the foundation for making improvements in the coming weeks. I thought it would be best to discuss in person."

"I was excited to see your invite. I've been starting to feel more and more empowered as we move through the steps."

"I'm glad to hear that. How did it go yesterday?"

Lauren described the conversation she'd had with Gene regarding her strengths and weaknesses.

Claire was pleased with her progress. "With that information, you'll need to work with Justin to develop a training plan and determine your coaching needs. Back in the *Define* step, I mentioned how your manager is one of your suppliers. Well, training and coaching are two of the most important things a manager supplies an employee," Claire explained.

"However, I want to make sure I'm clear about something here. As an employee, you are ultimately responsible for reaching your full potential. You must seek help when and where you need it. Your boss' responsibility is to both you and the company. By helping you reach your full potential, naturally, the company benefits, which is partly why I'm mentoring you. The other part is that I really think you can succeed," she said with a smile.

"Working with Justin is getting easier, so I feel more comfortable asking him for training, although I'm still a bit hesitant," Lauren acknowledged with a grin.

"I expect it'll feel that way for a while. But now we need to move on to the rest of *Analyze*. First, we need to determine what part of your work is value added versus non-value added."

"What do you mean? All my work is value added."

"The definition of value added work is work you do that the customer is willing to pay for. Obviously, fixing hardware and software errors that shouldn't have occurred in the first place is not something the customer wants to pay for. As you know, the Texas plant has been working on the hardware issues, and I've just started working with the IT department on software errors.

"As an individual, where have you been wasting time in non-value added ways? An example of this would be disorganized files. Sounds simple, but do you ever spend 5 minutes looking for a file on your computer?"

"Yeah of course. I can spend as much as 10 minutes looking for a file. Sometimes, it takes so long I just give up," Lauren responded.

"This is a common issue, but it's something the customer does not want to pay for. That means it's non-value added. Organizing files on your computer would eliminate this waste," Claire explained.

Claire asked Lauren if the Account Management department had a standardized method for organizing files. "If they have one, I am not aware of it. I just made one up that worked for me," Lauren responded.

"Disorganized files exemplify how a lack of standardization creates non-value added activity. With everyone creating their own file management system, it takes longer to find files."

Lauren agreed. "That's definitely something I can fix with Justin's help."

"Good. I've just given you an improvement idea that could be implemented. This would help with the metric *number of implemented individual improvements per month.*"

"The time I spend solving customer complaints is definitely non-value added work. Tech Support is more efficient than I am at handling those complaints. However, I can be more effective by getting to the root cause of the problem." Lauren added.

"Perfect. When an employee finds the root cause and implements a permanent solution, they free up time to focus on value-added work. What can you do that adds value for the customer?"

"Honestly, I'm not sure how to add value. Perhaps if I better understood Symbay's business strategies and challenges, I might be able to find ways," Lauren confessed. She had just had an "Aha!" moment. She got more excited and started to talk faster.

"I need to think bigger!" she exclaimed.

Claire was pleased with Lauren's response. "I'm glad to hear you thinking proactively. It'll take some effort to understand where non-value added work is occurring. "

Lauren could tell where this was going. "So I'll need to analyze customer data, most likely with Justin?"

"You got it. While you're analyzing that data, not only do you need to figure out what waste is occurring, you need to figure out *why* it's happening. You'll need to work with Justin to identify the root causes of waste."

"When you said I was being reactive, that meant I was just solving problems as they occurred. This is a more proactive activity—going past the problems to figure out what's really causing them," Lauren said.

"That's absolutely correct. It's this kind of problem solving that leads to long-term improvements.

"Last but not least, make sure you can *verify* the causes you identify," Claire explained. "By direct observation and dialogue with your customers, you can gather data to support your conclusions.

This is where the groundwork you've laid building relationships with your customers will come in handy.

"And that's the *Analyze* step. All the improvements you make to your job within the next couple of weeks will come from the groundwork you've laid here."

Lauren couldn't wait to begin analyzing. She was more than ready to make real changes. "Great! Thank you so much for setting up this meeting. I can't wait to get started."

Claire was pleased with Lauren's eagerness. With the *Analyze* step explained, Claire ended the meeting and made plans to review Lauren's findings after yoga on Friday.

· · · · ·

Excited with the challenge of digging into her role, Lauren sat down at her desk to prepare the data to review with Justin. She now had a wealth of information from which to pull. The trick was making sense of it all.

Symbay's primary problems were the technical issues, so Lauren decided to start there. She pulled the data from Tech Support on how many complaint calls they'd received over the last six months. During that period, the number of Symbay users had grown significantly. The number of complaints had also steadily increased.

"Much as I hate to admit it, Justin's right; I need to send all of these calls to Tech Support," she concluded.

She then reviewed how quickly complaints were resolved. According to the data from Tech Support, the average amount of time was 36 hours. Lauren knew the expectations set by Max Potential's salesmen was 24 hours. With this discrepancy, Lauren identified a significant cause of diminished trust between the two companies.

When she had gone through the data, she noticed how frequently users were calling with technical issues and calling again after 24 hours when their issue hadn't been resolved.

It seemed that Tech Support hadn't been able to keep up with the influx in technical issues. Lauren needed a way to minimize complaints while ensuring that resolution times consistently stayed under 24 hours.

For the rest of the afternoon, Lauren pored over descriptions of the technical issues. She systematically grouped them into categories based on type of complaint. For the most frequent complaints, she pulled actual call sheet examples. With six months of data to examine, it took several hours to complete.

"Oh my gosh, no wonder no one's figured out what's wrong with Symbay. This is so tedious," she complained to herself. "At least I'll have what I need for my discussion with Justin tomorrow." It might be hard work, but she knew it would be worth it.

Nearly unable to think, she got up from her desk to grab a coffee. "I don't even care if this keeps me up tonight. I've got to get through the rest of this data analysis before my meeting."

With that, she dove back into the data. This time she focused on the training processes.

"How many training sessions have we actually provided to Symbay?"

She looked at her calendar to see how many training sessions she had conducted. When she first started as an Account Coordinator, she had done training sessions every month. In the past three months, she'd only held a training session when new users were added.

She then compiled the survey results from her last training session. She identified specific quotes Justin might find insightful and averaged the overall rating of the training.

The results were worse than she expected. The employees gave the effectiveness of the training a 3 out of 5. When asked how prepared they felt to use the MaxPTs, they gave a paltry 2.5 out of 5.

"Something is clearly wrong here. When was this training developed?"

She looked through the company's records stored on the intranet. The training materials had been uploaded almost three years ago.

"I'll have to talk to Justin about this."

The last thing to prepare was information on how Symbay was customizing and using the MaxPTs. Luckily, Symbay's data usage was recorded and accessible. Lauren could see which apps Symbay used and how many users in each department had the apps installed. She pulled this information and compared it to MaxPTs' default settings.

She then made a list of all the functionalities the MaxPTs had for Symbay employees. With this information, she could make sure the MaxPTs were doing what Symbay needed. Her only problem was she did not yet know Symbay's business enough to evaluate if the devices were customized effectively. To do that, she'd have to continue building her understanding of their business.

By the end of the day, she had a wealth of information to review with Justin. She could give him a full picture of technical issues, training, and customization.

Lauren left her desk feeling excited about the insights she'd uncovered and satisfied with the work she'd done.

• • • • •

When it came time to meet with Justin, Lauren was well prepared. Not only did she have the right data to analyze, she also had a more comfortable rapport with Justin since she had begun fostering the relationship.

As she entered the conference room, Justin was more relaxed than he had been in the initial meeting about Phillip's email.

"Alright, here we go," she thought.

She confidently began the meeting. "I've been analyzing our relationship with Symbay and wanted your help to complete my analysis. Before we get to that, I'd like to discuss my training needs."

She asked for Justin's support developing her strengths and improving her weaknesses. To Lauren's surprise, Justin was eagerly willing to help.

"I think it's smart to work together to improve your strategic thinking about the customer's needs," he responded. He suggested an online insurance industry course to help Lauren learn more about Symbay's business. He also said the company could purchase a subscription to an online insurance magazine.

Lauren felt this was a great start. "I will dive into both of these to learn more. Would you be available for a monthly meeting to coach me?" she asked. She had remembered Gene's comment about Justin's proficiency for strategy and knew he would be a great resource.

"That's a great idea," Justin responded. "After our meeting, just send me an invite."

"Regarding the Symbay account, there are a lot of improvements to make. The question we need to answer in this meeting is, 'Why is Symbay having so many problems?'

"I couldn't agree more," he responded.

She explained she'd been routing the calls to Tech Support as Justin had requested, but he wanted to know why she was getting so many calls in the first place.

"Even if you're sending calls to Tech Support, that's still wasted time spent answering those calls. Why are people calling you specifically?" he asked.

Lauren hadn't thought about that. "Most of the MaxPT information within Symbay is disseminated by Stan. When someone has an issue, they likely ask him who to call. I suppose because he and I have a solid relationship, he tells them to call me."

"Then it's time to reset expectations. Symbay needs to be aware of our customer complaint process. We need to *standardize* how they're contacting us," Justin determined.

Lauren would have to create a consistent way for Symbay employees to solve their issues and communicate it clearly to her customers.

"Did you also get a chance to look at how long it takes to resolve technical issues?" he asked.

"Yes, it looks like we're averaging 36 hours," she responded. She knew he wouldn't be happy with that answer.

"We promise them 24 hours. That number is unacceptable," Justin stated. "How do we get it down?"

The data showed that Tech Support received an average of 50 service calls per week per 1000 users. They were simply inundated with customer calls. Lauren needed to stop spending time solving customer complaints and figure out the root causes of those problems.

"To see the causes of these issues, I went through data from Tech Support and noticed complaints have been increasing—no surprise there. Then I went through the data to see what they'd been calling about."

She laid her findings on the table. Together, they looked through the technical issues to determine which complaints were due to software malfunctions, hardware problems, user error, and improper setup.

The first thing that stood out was the MaxPTs locking users out of the system or people seemingly forgetting their passwords. She was all too familiar with this problem from her experience handling complaints. She knew a quick workaround and could fix it for the client, so she normally took care of these without forwarding them to Tech Support.

Seeing the data, it became apparent how much time this issue wasted.

Justin wanted to know more. "Do we know why this continues to happen? Is this a bug in our system or is Symbay making the mistake? If we solve this issue, it would cut down on calls significantly."

Lauren agreed to look into this issue and see if she could solve it.

They moved on to other types of technical issues. The bucket of complaints from user error was slightly larger than the others.

"If user error is leading to so many complaints, we might need to look at how we're training users and what kind of information we're providing. It's probably also important to set up the devices more intuitively," Justin remarked. "This will help us understand the cause of wasted time spent resolving issues."

Lauren jotted this down along with the rest of the "to do" items she'd already garnered from the meeting. It was now time to move on to training.

They looked at the training data and discussed how training session requests had declined. Justin noticed that the number of service calls had no correlation with users being trained. It appeared people were having just as many problems whether they had the training or not.

"It seems our training isn't working very well for Symbay," Lauren postulated. "We don't customize it, correct? There should be a marked difference in their ability to use the MaxPTs depending on who's had training." Lauren was having a breakthrough.

"Plus, when I took a survey at the end of my training session, people did not seem to feel comfortable using the devices. They rated the effectiveness of the training a 3 out of 5." Lauren had more than enough information to verify the cause of waste.

"We're spending too much time fixing the MaxPTs because we don't properly train Symbay employees in the first place," Justin said.

Lauren had uncovered a type of waste in her processes.

"Let me pull up our training materials." She brought them up and compared what the training materials said about the MaxPTs, and how Symbay employees actually used the devices.

"It looks like there's a ton of information that doesn't apply. I noticed this during our training session as well. I bet that's confusing for our client," Lauren said. She had honed in on one of the problems leading to technical issues.

They looked through the training manual together and analyzed what was and wasn't useful. Much of the content was completely irrelevant for Symbay. They decided Lauren would customize the training materials to better suit their needs.

"Going back to your comment on setting up the devices, I gathered information on what apps our customers are using and what kind of functionality they require," Lauren explained. "From the customer complaints, it seems our users are trying to get the devices to function in a way that differs from how they're set up."

"How do they need to be set up?" he asked.

"I think that's something I need to understand better. I'll learn more about Symbay's business so we can customize the training and the devices to deliver exactly what they need."

Justin was pleased she had located the source of the problem and had a plan to fix it.

It was also apparent that Symbay users were not using many of the apps provided during the initial setup.

"People are distracted by unnecessary functions, so they make mistakes when they use the device. This would also explain why Phillip feels they aren't providing value," she said.

Justin knew she was right—and Lauren had the data to prove it.

"Phew. That's a lot of information we've covered," she assessed.

Lauren felt it had been an incredibly productive meeting. She was pleasantly surprised by how willing Justin had been to help her. He seemed impressed by the data she had found and organized. He tended to respond well to concrete information.

"I'm glad you took the initiative to walk through all of this. Now that we have this information, we'll need to make steps to solve the problems we've uncovered and communicate it to the client. It sounds like you need to talk more with Stan and Phillip," Justin commented. For the first time in a while, he was optimistic about the Symbay account.

Lauren agreed, and let him know she'd write up the notes from their meeting to make sure they were in agreement about how to move forward. As she walked out of his office, she felt ready to move on to the *Improve* step.

Based on what Justin had said, Lauren knew that Claire needed to understand the root causes of complaints from the customer so she could deal with them in other areas of the business. Lauren drafted an email, specifically listing the unnecessary complexities of the device causing issues.

"I'd love to fix this, but it's really a question of how the devices are engineered, and that's not something I can fix." Lauren was proud of herself for knowing what her responsibilities were and, just as importantly, what weren't.

· · · · ·

Claire was satisfied with the progress Lauren was making, and it was time for Claire to practice what she preached. She'd trained Lauren to build relationships with her customers, and now she needed to do the same. She'd set up a meeting with Phillip, the VP from Symbay.

To coach Lauren in the next step of improvement, she needed to have a high-level discussion with Phillip to find out Symbay's strategic goals and pain points. As the COO of Max Potential, it was her job to know the customer as well.

She'd invited Phillip out for lunch to introduce herself and to discuss Symbay's business needs. When she arrived, Phillip had already sat down and ordered a glass of iced tea.

As Claire approached, she planned how she would begin the conversation. After she made her introduction and sat down, she began on a personal note by asking Phillip how long he'd been in Dayton.

"Oh, I've lived in Dayton my whole life. I think it's a great city. I've always wanted to make it an even better place for the people who live here, which is why I love my job with Symbay. I think we have a great platform to make a difference."

"That's interesting. How does Symbay go about doing that?"

Phillip paused. "We're not doing as much as we'd like. We're identifying ways to become more integrated into the Dayton community. We notice our employees are more motivated when they're closer to the community members for whom we provide insurance and they can anticipate consumer needs."

Claire saw an opportunity to provide value with MaxPTs. She made a mental note of the pain point Phillip had just divulged.

They continued chatting about their personal lives. Claire told Phillip about her experiences coming to Dayton and her background in the tech industry. She could sense Phillip relaxing into the conversation as Claire opened up to him.

Eventually, Claire guided the conversation to more professional topics. She asked Phillip what he was looking for with respect to Symbay's relationship with Max Potential.

"In the short term, I need to see a sharp decline in the amount of issues we're having. It's causing too much rework within our departments. Our employees are frustrated with a system that doesn't work seamlessly. There's confusion and an unwillingness to fully commit to using the MaxPTs.

"That said, we have noticed a marked improvement in the hardware issues we were having. The new MaxPTs are running better than before."

Claire had worked with the Texas plant for the last three months on The 5 Disciplines, and was pleased it was positively affecting her customer. "I'm so glad to hear you say that. We've implemented a new improvement process and are seeing much better quality."

"We've certainly noticed," Phillip replied. "In the long term, I need the MaxPTs to make life easier for employees. It should free up time so they can be more productive. Instead, our progress has stalled as more people have started using them. "

Claire was highly grateful for the insight Phillip had provided. She now knew the reasons behind his first email expressing doubts about the MaxPTs.

As the lunch went on, she gained a clear understanding about the challenges of the insurance industry and Phillip's goals for Symbay's future. She paid close attention so she could coach Lauren during the *Improve* step.

She opened up to Phillip about where she wanted to take Max Potential. "My focus is to make sure we are doing everything we can to support your company's goals. At this moment, what is Symbay's primary focus for future growth?"

Phillip seemed pleased with her approach to build the relationship between Symbay and Max Potential. He explained Symbay's strategy to cut costs by maximizing efficiencies. Symbay's mission was to provide the most affordable insurance possible to their customers. By streamlining their operations, they could pass those savings onto customers, increase profitability and gain market share. Like Max Potential, much of their rework was due to poor training, lack of standardization, and work process complexity.

Claire was glad to understand the deeper roots of Symbay's perspective. "As we continue to address your initial concerns and solidify our partnership, I'll work with our team to make sure the MaxPTs help you achieve your business goals."

Phillip told her that he felt better about the MaxPTs after she had listened to his concerns and made clear her desire to provide solutions. But he knew that only time would tell if Max Potential could carry through with their promises.

ANALYZE STEP SUMMARY

The following questions can be asked in the *Analyze* step to help answer the question *"How do I analyze my job?"*

What are my strengths and weaknesses?

Before you can improve your skills, you must identify the areas in which you excel and which can be improved.

- Lauren had a strong technical knowledge of the MaxPTs and great people skills. She needed to learn to think strategically about her customer's needs.

What are my training and coaching needs?

No one is born with the knowledge to do their job. Everyone must be trained. You then must get feedback from customers, managers and colleagues on what you are doing right and what you can improve.

- Lauren had a discussion with Justin on her training and coaching needs based upon an analysis of her strengths and weaknesses.

What types of non-value added work or waste are in my processes?

Most non-value added work comes in two forms: *rework* in the form of not doing things right the first time (poor quality); and *wasted time* in the form of waiting for materials, information, etc.

- Complaints from Stan had been increasing, so Lauren met with Justin to analyze complaints. Most of them were rework related to the customer not knowing how to use MaxPT.

What are the causes of my waste?

One of the most common root causes of rework is poor training, lack of standardization, and too much complexity. This leads to confusion and inefficiencies.

- Lauren identified four categories of waste: hardware issues, customer complaints, training, and customization. She and Justin analyzed the training data and noticed attendance of the online training had decreased. The satisfaction scores were 2.5 out of 5, which was lower than the 4.0 historical average.

Can I verify the causes?

It is important to gather data and/or verify by direct observation and dialogue with your customers.

- The data showed the training was thorough, but did not address the prevailing issues with Symbay's service calls. Lauren and Stan also talked to recent users of the training who verified this hypothesis. The complexity issue is a long-term problem that product design will need to resolve. Claire will have to decide how to handle this issue.

4

IMPROVE

How Do I Improve?

STEP 4 IMPROVE

"Ahh, it's finally Friday," Lauren thought as the clock hit five. She pushed her chair away from her desk and stood to pack her things. She couldn't wait to review her *Analyze* findings with Claire after yoga.

Yoga was especially calming that evening. After class, Claire and Lauren found a table to chat.

"Yoga and Juicing night once again," Claire reflected. "I have to say, this is one of the best parts of my week."

"I agree. It's so nice to finish the week with great yoga and relaxation after work. Also, I can't wait to learn more about The 5 Disciplines."

Claire smiled. She was happy Lauren was so eager to reach her full potential. "Before we start talking about the next step, tell me how *Analyze* went. Did you answer the remaining questions with Justin?"

"Oh my gosh, yes. I pulled data from every source I could find, and we walked through it together. His help was awesome in figuring out the root causes of our problems."

Claire was pleased. "I'm glad to hear that. It seems Justin has become an asset to your role instead of the stressful presence he'd been before. So tell me your answers to the *Analyze* step."

Lauren laid the write-up she'd prepared out on the table. While they sipped glasses of the green apple, carrot and vegetable juice mix, she walked Claire through the discoveries she'd made both on her own and with Justin.

Based on her analysis, Lauren explained she'd uncovered four buckets from which she could improve her job performance: complaints process, training, improper customization, and higher-level strategic issues. Each of her improvements would be directed towards one of those four buckets.

Claire was impressed. "This is exactly what the *Analyze* step is designed to achieve. Now that you've thoroughly verified the causes of your non-value added work, it's time to talk about *Improve*.

"The *Define*, *Measure*, and *Analyze* steps were all about planning. The *Improve* step is all about doing," Claire explained. "Do you remember in the *Measure* step when I mentioned the metric *number of individual improvements implemented per month*?"

"I do remember that. I was wondering when it was going to come back around," Lauren answered.

"Well, now is the time. Today we're going to talk about which improvements you're going to make. Each month, I would like you to review with Justin how many improvements you've implemented. Consistent improvement maintained over time will help you achieve full potential. The *Improve* Step is ultimately about asking the question, "How do I improve?"

HOW DO I IMPROVE?

"I'd like to start the *Improve* step by asking how you can improve your relationships at work."

"From what I've learned over the last couple of weeks, relationships are central to getting anything done. First of all, building a relationship with you has exposed me to The 5 Disciplines, and that's completely changing the way I operate." Lauren said. "Applying open and honest communication to my relationship with Justin has allowed me to understand how to speak his language and see where he's coming from. My plan for continuing to improve relationships at work is to build the personal aspects while also keeping my promises."

"That's exactly right. You've got that one in the bag. Make sure you continue to build all of your relationships: the ones with your internal customers, external customers, and suppliers. Improving those relationships will be crucial to improving your role overall." Claire responded.

"I can do that," said Lauren. She felt like she was starting to get the hang of this.

Claire continued, "What are your work goals? Within The 5 Disciplines, 'goals' has a distinct meaning; it refers to the specific objectives you would like to achieve this year or within a specific period. The ones you list must directly pertain to your own metrics, from the *Measure* step, and your department's."

Lauren loved writing goals. She was the type of person who always had a list of goals she was working towards. This wouldn't be a problem for her. Although, given Claire's explanation of goals within The 5 Disciplines, she knew she'd have to be more disciplined about the ones she set.

"Based on what you've taught me about keeping the customer at the center, I think the first goal I have will be based on what is most important to Stan and Phillip. That's minimizing technical issues."

Claire agreed. "That's a good place to start. Try to quantify that goal so you can measure your progress against a concrete metric."

"Based on the information I found, we're averaging 50 issues per week per 1000 users." She stopped to ponder what would be an achievable goal. "Half. That's what I want to do. I want to cut that number by half in six months."

"That's a pretty lofty goal, but I can guarantee if you hit that number, it would go a long way to repair the relationship with Symbay."

Lauren had faith in herself. "I think I can do it. 25 technical issues a week is in reach, and if we could lower the number by that much, our Tech Support team would be able to quickly resolve issues, hopefully within 24 hours."

"What others do you have? I like to have at least three at any given time."

"The other big initiative I want to resolve is our training processes. Hopefully, that will help us reduce our technical issues.

"When I reviewed the surveys I administered at the recent training session, attendees rated their preparedness to use the MaxPTs a 2.5 out of 5. That number should be much higher. After I redo the training materials, I'd like to reach an average of 4 out 5."

Claire could get on board with that. "That's a reasonable expectation."

"And last, I'd really like to focus on my ability to think more strategically. I'm not sure exactly how to build a metric around that, but I would like to improve my ability to understand the customer's needs."

"Not every goal has to have a metric. With this last goal, I think it's perfectly reasonable to challenge yourself to act more proactively with the customer. As you grow your skills in this area, it'll become clear when you're providing value by consulting your customer instead of just reacting to problems."

Lauren was pleased. She had three clear goals she could use.

Claire moved on. "Based on what you know now, what are your ideas for improvement? These are the ideas that will help you achieve your goals. Any idea that will help you do your job better is a valid idea for improvement," Claire explained.

Lauren took a deep breath and began laying out her ideas. "Starting with the technical issues, I'd like to meet with my previous Tech Support supervisor every other week. If I can figure out why users are calling in with complaints, I can figure out how to get to the root cause of those complaints and solve them proactively."

"Excellent," Claire said. "There's a helpful principle I like to use when solving problems. Have you ever heard of the Pareto principle?"

"I think I have. Justin's mentioned it before. Something to do with 80/20, but that's all I remember," Lauren answered.

"You're on the right track. The Pareto Principle says that 20% of something is responsible for 80% of the results. For example, with the technical issues you're having, instead of focusing on all of the problems, try to find the 20% that are causing 80% of the issues."

"It's interesting you say that. We talked about the ways we want to curb technical issues, and we noticed user error is a big one. People simply don't know how to use the devices. We reviewed the training materials and noticed it's completely outdated. I'd like to work with the team that created the materials and revise them for Symbay."

"Brilliant. What other improvement ideas do you have?"

"I'd also like to spend at least three uninterrupted hours a week researching Symbay, the insurance market they serve, and the larger concerns of the insurance industry so I can customize the devices to serve their needs," Lauren declared.

But Claire had some additional information that would help Lauren provide value to Symbay.

"Before we go any further, I want to ask what you believe Symbay is using the MaxPTs for. Why do they continue to invest in our device?"

Lauren felt like she should know the answer. She began to fidget nervously. She normally assumed this question was for the sales team to understand. She was in charge of making sure Symbay employees were satisfied with the devices. At least that's how she'd felt before she began working on The 5 Disciplines.

"Um, wow. I suppose it's for the same reason most customers use our devices. They keep everything consolidated for employees. They run well…" Lauren answered hesitantly.

"You're right. Those are selling points we list on our website, but I'm trying to get you to think about the unique needs and perspective of the customer.

"This week, I met with Phillip, because like you, I wasn't entirely sure what Symbay expected from the MaxPTs. Listening to the voice of the customer is the fuel that drives all of our improvement efforts," said Claire.

Claire explained Phillip's vision to become more integrated into the communities they serve in order to help employees connect with customers. She also explained Symbay's vision to cut customer costs and how they planned to do so.

"With that in mind, what customer-centric improvements can you implement?"

"I guess one of the reasons Symbay is having issues using the MaxPTs is that the devices aren't customized for their needs. If I can learn about Symbay's business, I could advise them on customization. I've already set up a bi-weekly meeting with Stan and reviewed data on which apps Symbay isn't using."

"I think it will also be a good idea to sit down with Phillip. Once we've implemented your improvements, I will set up an introduction and meeting."

"That would be great. I know I need to repair the relationship, but I wasn't sure how. That would help a lot."

"Perfect. Now, all of your improvements fit within the four main buckets of problems Symbay is experiencing. How do you plan to implement your ideas?" Claire elaborated, "It seems you already have an idea of who you're going to work with to implement your ideas. You're ahead of the curve on this one."

"Yes, I don't think I'll have any choice but to lean on other departments: Tech Support, Training, IT, and, just like in the other steps, Justin."

"I'm glad you're learning how to use the partnerships you've built. Improvement ideas often require planning. When you meet with each of the departments, make sure to lay out concrete steps to implement your improvement ideas. By bringing others on board with your vision, you increase the likelihood of success.

"The *Improve* step will take some time to implement. For that reason, let's regroup two weeks from now. That'll give us time to review your improvements and prepare to meet with Phillip. I'll set that meeting up for the following Friday."

"Perfect! Three weeks ago when I received Phillip's email, I had no idea how I would handle it. I was completely overwhelmed. But with The 5 Disciplines, I feel so much more capable to take control of my job and the situation. I think the next couple of weeks will start to prove to Phillip that the MaxPTs are the right choice for Symbay."

Claire could see The 5 Disciplines were doing exactly what they needed to do. Lauren had asked herself the right questions and was in a position to function more effectively than before.

The women toasted to another step reviewed. They enjoyed the relaxing Friday night, but Lauren was more ready than ever to jump into action Monday.

• • • • •

On Monday morning, Lauren remembered Claire's comment about making concrete plans to implement her improvement ideas. She wrote down her four improvement buckets, her improvement ideas for each, and the steps she would take to implement them.

The previous couple of days, Lauren found she had more time on her hands. Since she no longer took Tech Support calls, she had enough time to think proactively.

The first issue to fix was the amount of technical issues Symbay was experiencing and the lengthy resolution time. She dialed the number for her former supervisor in Tech Support, Garrett, asking him if he was free to talk. He agreed to meet later that morning.

They found a small meeting room in which to discuss the tech results. "Thanks so much for meeting with me. I'm in the process of making improvements to the Symbay MaxPTs and I wanted to talk about how we can work together to decrease the amount of technical issues they're experiencing."

Garrett looked happy to hear her say that. "That would really help our team. They call us with a whole lot of issues."

"Right. I didn't realize just how many issues they'd been experiencing until I dug into the numbers. I've come up with a couple of solutions I think will help."

"Great, I'd love to hear them," Garrett responded enthusiastically.

"From my end, I plan to customize the training and create a customized design for the devices. I'd like to set up a bi-weekly meeting between you and me to discuss the most common issues Symbay is experiencing. Your team has better access to that information than I do. If I know what's going wrong, I can dig into the root causes and come up with a permanent solution to reduce the issues from recurring.

"It will also help me gain insight into our average resolution time. We initially discussed aiming for 24 hours for Symbay, but it seems our average is 36. If you and I can solve some of these issues, it will certainly lower the turnaround time."

"I like that idea."

"While we're on the subject, are there any issues right now that stand out as common occurrences?"

Garrett immediately had an answer. "Yes, Symbay keeps getting locked out of their devices. I don't know why it's happening. We can fix it pretty easily by manually resetting the passwords on our end, but that doesn't keep it from happening again."

"Interesting," Lauren responded. "I'm aware of this issue. How often does it happen?"

"Oh, we get at least a couple of those calls a week."

"I'll look into that and figure out why it's happening. Maybe IT can help. I'm planning to meet with them later this week.

"So with things like that, if I can fix them, your team will be less inundated with calls and more likely to achieve our target 24-hour resolution time."

"I think that's doable if we can reduce the number of calls," Garrett said.

"I'm glad to hear that. Are you able to automatically send me data each week so I can keep tabs on how many calls we're receiving and what our turnaround time is?"

"Yeah, we can easily set that up."

"That would be great. The second thing I want to mention is from this point forward, I will be sending every complaint call your way. In the past, I've handled some of the issues myself. I need to focus on other priorities, so I won't be taking them anymore. The customer will be better served by your team's efficient and consistent handling of the issues."

Garrett smiled. "I think that's a good idea. That way we can standardize how to resolve the common issues we receive."

With their new plan in place, they parted ways and planned to meet again in two weeks.

When she sat down at her desk, Lauren scheduled a joint meeting with Justin and IT. She needed to figure out why Symbay users were getting locked out of their devices as well as how to customize the devices to best serve their needs.

While she was at her desk, she sent Stan an email asking if he would be available to sit down over coffee to discuss the MaxPTs. He responded by saying he could meet tomorrow morning.

"Perfect," she said to herself. "We're going to get Symbay back on track."

• • • • •

When Stan arrived at Press coffee shop the next morning, Lauren had already sat down with a list of prepared questions. She knew exactly what she wanted to achieve. Client meetings were always a bit intimidating, but she liked the opportunity to build her client interaction skills.

She warmly greeted Stan and engaged in some pleasant small talk. When they'd settled in, she explained that the purpose of the meeting was to discuss technical issues, training, and how Symbay was using the devices.

"We've done some analysis and noticed that a lot of the complaint calls are being sent directly to me. In the past, I'd done some of the tech support, but I'm routing all of that to our Tech Support team so I can focus on the larger issues. Are you able to encourage people to call Tech Support exclusively for these issues?" she asked.

"Yes, we can make that happen. We've worked so closely that you seemed like the natural point person. I'm happy to send an email with the new information."

Lauren then dove into how Symbay was using the devices. She knew it would be a long, and possibly tedious, conversation, but it was an important one to have. She pulled one of the MaxPTs from her briefcase.

"I'd like to walk through each of the apps Symbay employees use. We pulled device data and noticed your team isn't using some of the apps that come pre-loaded onto the device. The inclusion of unnecessary functions might be causing confusion."

Stan realized she was right. "Yeah, I've noticed there are a lot of apps I don't use or I don't fully use. For instance, the chat functionality is a decent app, but we have an intranet chat function we already use. It just doesn't make sense to use two chat platforms."

Lauren was surprised. She had no idea. "That's great information. We can remove our chat function and see if we can pre-load Symbay's existing system onto the devices."

"That'll make things much easier for our team. I know some people have complained that they can't figure out how to load Symbay's chat app onto the MaxPTs, so they just don't do it. That means only some of our employees are using it, so not everyone is available to chat with the people who have figured it out."

Bing! Lauren felt like a light bulb had gone off. "That's such a simple fix. Yes!" she celebrated in her mind.

They spent the next half-hour looking through each and every app, deciding what Symbay needed and what could be deleted. Lauren then decided to think ahead.

"Regarding daily operations, is there anything Symbay has difficulty doing? I'll be meeting with our IT team this week, and I'd like to understand if there are any issues the MaxPTs can help solve."

"We can certainly do that. We'd like to engage our employees socially within our company, but we've had trouble informing them about upcoming events. We have a great culture, but on numerous occasions people say they missed an event or don't feel connected to other employees."

This was exactly the information Lauren was looking for. It could help her figure out a way to provide additional value using the MaxPTs. "I know we have some additional social and community networking apps we haven't explored for Symbay. I'll check on those this week."

Stan never thought to use the MaxPTs to help with the problem he'd described. "That would be fantastic for our team!"

Claire's proactive, consultative approach seemed to be working. There was only one thing left to discuss.

"I'd like to talk about training. It seems our training materials aren't as helpful as they could be. I've begun to reevaluate them. Would you be open to distributing updated training manuals?"

"Yes, I would be open to that. Whatever helps our team. I trust your guidance, especially after the improvements we've discussed today. Just let me know how I can help."

Lauren was overjoyed to hear Stan say he trusted her judgment. She let him know she'd keep him updated on their progress improving the training manuals.

Lauren sipped the last of her coffee. She expressed how happy she was they were able to meet. Stan agreed.

• • • • •

With insight from her meeting with Stan, Lauren gathered her things to meet with Justin and Ben from the IT team.

She walked into the conference room to see Justin sitting in his typical upright and rigid fashion, while Ben sat behind his computer barely looking up to acknowledge her. She wasn't used to working with IT, so she wasn't sure what to expect.

After they made introductions, Lauren began, "Today I'd like to discuss customizing Symbay's devices to better suit their needs. But first, I'd like to fix an issue that seems to keep happening to Symbay users. Based on my discussion with Tech Support, users are frequently getting locked out of their devices. When I was fielding these calls, I solved it by simply resetting the password as an admin on our side, but I'd like to figure out why it's happening in the first place."

Justin was impressed. This was the type of thinking he'd asked her to do in their first meeting after Phillip's email.

Ben walked them through the password setup system. They examined how the devices locked people out, but nothing explained why so many users were losing their passwords. They began to brainstorm why this kept happening.

Ben mentioned the password had to be reset every two months for security reasons. That sparked an idea in Lauren's mind.

"Are they being properly alerted when it's time to change their passwords? Is there a way to figure out what alerts have been sent?"

"Yeah, that's an easy one," Ben answered.

Together they looked at how many alerts were going to Symbay and noticed inconsistencies. It seemed that some Symbay employees weren't receiving notifications because of a bug in the alert system.

"Well, that's your problem," Ben said.

"How do we fix it?" Justin asked.

"That'll have to be sent to the development team. It's a code error. They can probably fix it pretty easily."

"Yes!" Lauren burst out. She couldn't contain her excitement. One solution, found.

Energized from their discovery, she was eager to move on to customizing the devices for Symbay.

She took Ben and Justin through the device usage Stan had explained to her. She showed them which apps were being used the most and which were largely being ignored.

With Justin's expertise on the Symbay account and on using the MaxPTs to deliver value, he helped them brainstorm new ways to customize the devices.

They made significant changes and documented the customizations that would help Symbay.

Lauren also brought up Symbay's focus on employee social engagement. "Is there any way we can connect Symbay employees with what's happening company-wide?"

They searched through the apps available, found one that was compatible with a company news app, and synced it with MaxPTs' calendar app. Everything would be centralized within the system Symbay was already familiar with.

Lastly, they reviewed the chat capabilities Stan had mentioned. Ben knew a way to install Symbay's existing chat app onto the MaxPTs, so this could become the universal way Symbay employees communicated over instant messaging.

The meeting lasted over an hour and a half. They had gone into the weeds and meticulously examined and customized the devices for Symbay's needs. Now they had a device that Lauren was confident could deliver the value Phillip was looking for.

Justin suggested she work with Stan to test the new setup. He knew from experience it was best to thoroughly test any new ideas before introducing them to a larger audience. Lauren agreed, and they concluded the meeting.

• • • • •

Lauren finally had time to sit down and tackle the rest of the improvements on her list. It seemed like an overwhelming task, so she started small.

"Alright, a simple thing I can do to improve my efficiency is to reorganize my files. Claire said to aim for standardization, so how can I create a consistent way of naming and storing my digital files?" she asked herself.

In Tech Support, the filing system had been instituted across the department, so Lauren simply followed the guidelines she was given. In Account Services, though, she was saving files onto her computer ad hoc. With no experience creating an organized system, she needed to research best practices to get some ideas.

After examining several examples online, Lauren generated some simple parameters that could help her stay organized and cut down the time retrieving files, thus reducing non-value added work. This simple change seemed miniscule, but in the grand scheme of things, it would help Lauren generate greater value added output.

"One improvement, implemented. Now for the hard part: the training manual. I guess I'll just start reading the existing manual and make notes along the way," she strategized.

After an hour of reviewing, she had tweaks, but wasn't having any major breakthroughs. Then she remembered Claire's advice to build her improvements from the insights gained in the *Analyze* step.

Suddenly, she had an idea. "Why don't we build the training around the most common types of service calls we're receiving? We have all the information right in front of us. The new training could focus on that," Lauren exclaimed.

"Better yet, why not create an online tutorial instead of sending them to a day-long seminar? About 80% of the complaints we receive are around a core set of issues. That's what we'll build the training around. Cutting out the rest will save an entire day's worth of training," Lauren said, remembering Claire's comments about the Pareto Principle. She was happy she had found a way to cut down on time.

After talking to Stan, Lauren knew what needed to be in the training. "I can collaborate with Justin to build the training module based on customer needs."

"Now I also know the advanced functionalities that people in different departments will use. Maybe I can create a basic document and provide supplemental pages for more advanced usage. Then no one will have to look through irrelevant material, since that leads to confusion."

Lauren was having breakthroughs left and right. The old material was outdated and she had information from the *Analyze* step to fix it.

Maybe there was a better way to train new users.

She pushed her chair out from her desk and let it roll her into the hall. She peeked into Gene's cubicle to see if he was there. Sure enough, he was sitting quietly, typing away.

"Hey Gene, do you have a minute?" she called to him.

"Yeah, what's up?"

"I know for the accounts you handle you do all your training in person, but have you ever done the training online?" She was curious to see if there was an online training platform already set up.

"Actually, yeah. When I first started, we tried an online platform for one of our accounts, but we didn't have enough bandwidth to invest that much time into it," he responded.

"Could you show me where it is? I'm wondering if there's a way to put our training online for advanced users who need a refresher."

Gene walked over to Lauren's cubicle. He logged into Max Potential's online platform to show Lauren where the training was hosted.

When he left her cubicle, she went through the material. It was outdated and the interface was clunky. There was certainly potential in this solution, but it would take quite a bit of time and resources.

"Is there an easier way to make the new training documents available?" she wondered. Then she remembered that the MaxPTs had an excellent storage capacity.

"Why don't we just pre-load PDFs of the training manuals onto the MaxPTs? Or better yet, put it onto our system and provide an easy access link so we can see when someone downloads it onto their device? We'll direct new users to the training documents instead of defaulting to on-site training sessions. We'll also provide the option for on-site training as needed. During our bi-weekly meetings, Stan and I can discuss if anyone needs extra on-site training."

Lauren had to explore a couple of different options, but now she had one she was sure could work. She emailed Justin to let him know her idea.

He responded quickly, letting her know he thought the idea had potential.

With his approval, she started the process of rewriting the manuals. Her extensive technical knowledge and her understanding of how the devices needed to be customized for Symbay made her uniquely qualified to generate new training materials.

• • • • •

Lauren worked diligently creating the new documents. Throughout the week, whenever she had extra time, she worked on the training materials.

She didn't even stop on Friday. Claire had called her on Thursday to say she'd be out of town and unable to make it to yoga, so Lauren went to yoga by herself and headed straight home to continue working. Over the weekend she refined the documents so she could review a draft with Justin on Monday.

On Monday, she was anxious to show Justin the new training manual. It was finally time to reveal what she'd been working on.

She laid a printed copy on his desk. He looked up at her surprised at how quickly she had created a new manual.

"How much time did you spend on this?" he asked.

"Well, I got into it and couldn't stop. Let me walk you through it."

The new version was much shorter than the original manual. Because of her technical knowledge, Lauren was able to trim a great deal of unnecessary content to leave only the information a new user would need.

After walking Justin through the new material, she looked up to get a read on his response. He was still flipping through the pages. She began to feel a nervous sweat. "Oh come on, say something," she thought.

After what seemed like eternity, Justin moved his eyes from the pages and began to speak. "I really like what you've done here. You've streamlined the manual. It's much more relevant to Symbay. You're really taking ownership of this account, applying what you know and making it better."

Phew! Lauren let out a sigh of relief.

Justin continued. "I'd like to thoroughly review the entire document and send over comments. I see a few things I'd like to tweak, but overall, this looks great."

"Of course he has changes," Lauren thought with a smile. She had gotten to know Justin over the past couple of weeks and could now appreciate his attention to detail. In fact, it felt good having another set of eyes to contribute and provide feedback.

They continued discussing the logistics of the changes and how they could use the online platform to distribute it to Symbay. She remembered Claire's comment about being disciplined and making intentional plans to implement improvement ideas. Lauren made sure to agree on concrete next steps with Justin as they neared the end of the meeting.

Before they left, Justin took over. "I'm very happy with the initiative you've taken here. A couple of months ago, I was concerned about where we were with Symbay, but you've proven you can handle the responsibility. Have you thought about how to articulate these improvements to Phillip and the rest of the Symbay team?" he asked.

It was time to reveal how she'd turned the situation around. "Actually, I have. I'll be honest; when I got that email, I was unsure what would happen next and didn't know what to do.

"Luckily, I've been going to yoga at Speakeasy. It turns out that Claire, our new COO, practices there as well. Over the past month or so, we've been getting to know each other."

"Yes, I know. Claire has been coaching me too. We discussed your relationship once she told me the two of you met at yoga," said Justin.

Lauren was happy they were on the same page. "The process has completely redefined how I think about my job.

"Now, because of the relationship I've built with her, she would like to personally introduce me to Phillip. As part of her role as COO, she's been meeting the key contacts of our larger accounts and has already met with Phillip. Before I showed the client anything, I wanted to run it past you."

"I think the improvements you've made directly address Phillip's concerns, and it's time to let him know about the changes. If Claire has established a relationship with Phillip, she's the right person to help you do that. Just brief me after your meeting."

Lauren agreed. She made plans to meet with Justin the day before the meeting to review what she'd present to Phillip.

• • • • •

Her last post-yoga meeting with Claire seemed like a long time ago. Since then, Lauren had developed improvements that addressed every improvement bucket. She felt ready to present her work to Claire at their meeting on Wednesday.

As Claire walked in the room, she was excited to see how things had been going. "So, tell me, how did it go this past week and a half?"

"Excellent. I am fully prepared to meet with Phillip and demonstrate how we can address his concerns *and* show how we can provide significant value with the MaxPTs.

Lauren walked Claire through the solutions she'd developed and begun to implement. She presented her recent improvement activities.

Technical issues:
- Forward all customer complaints to Tech Support. Lauren is no longer available to resolve them.
- Stan will send an email instructing Symbay employees to submit complaints to the proper channels.
- Bi-weekly meetings with Tech Support have been scheduled to regularly review the most common complaints. Lauren would look for the root cause and develop potential solutions to improve the turnaround time for technical support calls.
- The number one complaint of users getting locked out of their devices has been resolved.

Customization
- Deleted unused apps from MaxPTs
- Installed apps to achieve new functionalities based on conversation with Stan
- Created an intuitive layout
- Apps to connect employees socially have been installed and integrated.
- New chat functionality has been added.

Training
- Training materials have been updated and simplified
- Department-specific training content has been added.

- Developed online training to replace introductory, on-site training
- Available for on-site training when requested

Strategy

- Bi-weekly meetings with Stan have been scheduled to address Symbay's pain points and make plans for improvement
- Taking a course on insurance and reading online insurance magazine
- Monthly coaching meetings with Justin have been scheduled.

Self-improvements

- Implementing a standardized filing system

"That's incredible – 17 improvements. How many improvements do you think the average employee at the average company makes per year?"

"I don't know. A whole year? My goal was 20. Maybe fifty?" Lauren guessed.

"It's actually only one. So 17 implemented improvements is huge. World class companies strive for 12 per year per employee," Claire said, overjoyed. "I can tell that you collaborated with multiple parties to arrange all of this. These improvements will change our relationship with Symbay. What a difference a month has made! How do you feel?"

"Empowered," Lauren answered with a grin. "For the first time since I started this position, I feel like I understand my job. I feel supported and capable."

"That's exactly what The 5 Disciplines is meant to do."

Claire had scheduled a meeting for her and Lauren to meet Phillip at Symbay on Friday. They worked together to create the agenda and assign who would present each item. Claire coached Lauren on her portion of the meeting.

"Are you nervous?" Claire asked. She'd developed a comfortable rapport with Lauren and knew she could ask those kinds of personal questions.

"A bit, but because I've spent so much preparation time, I feel ready. I'm confident Phillip will appreciate the work we've accomplished.

With that, they finished reviewing Lauren's improvements and finalized plans for the meeting on Friday. Lauren was finally ready to prove the value the MaxPTs could provide for Symbay.

• • • • •

She arrived at Symbay early for the meeting and waited at the front doors for the receptionist to let her in.

Claire hadn't yet arrived, so she sat in the lobby reviewing her presentation. Claire arrived just as Phillip entered the room. They shook hands and Claire introduced Lauren.

"It's great to meet you," he said to Lauren.

After brief introductions, they walked into a conference room and settled in. Lauren's heart was beating quickly, but she confidently began her presentation.

"Since we received your email expressing concerns about our devices, we've embarked on a thorough examination of how we can improve MaxPTs value to Symbay. This involved collecting data, talking with end users, reviewing training and strategically analyzing your business needs. By working closely with Stan and our internal departments, we've developed a set of improvements we can reasonably implement within the short term. We've also created a list of long-term solutions."

She walked Phillip through the analysis and improvements she'd executed over the previous month, while answering his periodic questions. When the presentation was over, Lauren anxiously awaited his response.

"Well, I have to say, this is exactly what we were looking for," Phillip said.

Lauren stayed professional on the outside, but in her mind, she was jumping for joy. "I'm glad to hear you say that."

"You've done some nice work creating solutions we never would have developed ourselves. The updates will help us achieve some of the goals we've been struggling with.

"The accounting department we added last month asked if they could use the MaxPTs. I'll be honest, I wasn't sure if it was the right decision to invest any further, given the concerns we were having. Given your new approach today, I think it would be great to introduce them to the devices. Would you be willing to take on a new department? After you've had a chance to test everything, of course."

"Absolutely!" Lauren exclaimed.

They discussed the needs of the new department. Lauren agreed to revise the training materials to address the functionalities required for their role.

Phillip asked a few more questions and they finished their meeting. He agreed to continue using the MaxPTs while monitoring progress to make sure they were indeed the right fit. Lauren had made significant progress in the relationship. However, she'd still have to prove to Phillip he'd made the right choice.

As Claire and Lauren walked out of Symbay to their cars, Claire grinned. "That's how you want to end a meeting—a happy customer and new business."

Lauren laughed. She couldn't have imagined a better outcome.

IMPROVE STEP SUMMARY

The following questions can be asked in the *Improve* step to help answer the question *"How do I improve?"*

How do I improve my relationships at work?

As in all personal relationships, spending quality time with people is the key to cultivating successful working relationships.

- Recently Lauren and Claire spent quality time together, resulting in an improved relationship. Also, Lauren's meetings (quality time) with Justin to resolve Symbay's problems have significantly improved their relationship. Lauren has begun to understand Justin's systematic and detailed approach to problem solving.

What are my work goals?

These are the objectives you are trying to achieve in a specific time frame. They should link to your work processes, metrics, and department goals.

Lauren had four goals:

1. Reduce the number of service calls from an average of 50 per week per 1000 users to 25.

2. Improve the training score from 2.5 to 4.0 out of 5.0.

3. Improve ability to understand her customer's needs in order to be more proactive.

4. Twenty implemented improvements this year.

What are my ideas for improvement?

These ideas often originate from the analysis performed in the *Analyze* step. Any idea that helps you do your job better or more efficiently is a valid idea for improvement.

- Lauren and Justin used the Pareto Principle to create improvement ideas and began redesigning the training to address the top five problems.

Do I need help implementing my improvement ideas?

Often improvement ideas require the help of other departments.

- Lauren met with Justin to discuss how to work with the IT and Training departments.

How do I implement my improvement ideas?

Complex improvement ideas require planning.

- Justin and Lauren met with the training supervisor and the Director of IT to develop a plan and coordinate the implementation of these improvements.

5

CONTROL

Am I Maintaining the Gains?

STEP 5 CONTROL

After the meeting with Phillip, Lauren debriefed Justin and began setting up the Symbay accounting department with their new MaxPTs. She planned to speak with Stan during their bi-weekly call to learn more about the department's needs. She would develop the training and customization from an informed, intentional perspective (a stark departure from her previous work). Like Claire, she was thinking strategically.

After work, she went to her Friday yoga class. This week, though, she and Claire didn't talk business. Instead they celebrated their recent success and enjoyed a relaxing Friday evening.

Claire let Lauren know the final step to go through was the *Control* step, but she wouldn't review it with Lauren for another month. It was important to allow the progress made in the first four steps to take effect so they could see the results.

When Monday came around, Lauren went straight to work. She knew what she was responsible for and had clear goals to achieve. Over the next couple of weeks, she continued to implement her improvements.

• • • • •

Claire checked in with Lauren periodically, but they hadn't been engaging in weekly training sessions like before. After a month, Claire decided it was time to go through the final step of The 5 Disciplines. On Wednesday, Claire found an open time in her schedule and stopped by Lauren's desk.

"Hey! Do you have 45 minutes before lunch to grab coffee? I'm excited to hear how things are going, and we need to go through the last step—*Control*."

"Yeah. Actually, I can go right now. Just came to a good stopping point."

"Perfect! Let me grab my purse, and I'll meet you up front."

They crossed the street to a nearby coffee shop. Over the last two months, they'd become friends. As they walked into the coffee shop, Lauren remembered something.

"Oh! I almost forgot. I'm throwing a third birthday party for my daughter Chloe this weekend. I'd love it if you could come."

Claire smiled. "That would be great."

Lauren gave her the details while they waited in line for coffee.

When they sat down, Claire asked Lauren to tell her how things had been going.

"Well, I pulled the data from Tech Support," Lauren started.

Claire jumped in. "Good news?"

"Good news," Lauren smiled. "Drumroll please... since we implemented our improvements, the service calls have been reduced by almost 30%!"

A 30% reduction in service calls for a client was huge. "That's tremendous! This positions us perfectly to start the *Control* step."

"I've been looking forward to the elusive 5th step of The 5 Disciplines. What is this one intended to do?"

"Well, the *Control* step is about maintaining your level of improvement over time. It's kind of like a diet. If you eat really healthy and achieve your target weight but then put it all back on in three months, what was the point? *Control* teaches you to ask yourself, *"Am I maintaining the gains?"*

AM I MAINTAINING THE GAINS?

"It's a step that is never fully completed. It would be like reviewing your personal goals and adjusting as needed. In the scientific method, this last step is what ensures continuous improvement.

"Would you say you're achieving your goals? To answer, you should review your goals monthly and determine if they are on the right track. There's a system I use that will help."

Claire pulled out a piece of paper from her briefcase. On it was a graph of goals with colors.

		CONTROL - Status											
IMPROVE		J	F	M	A	M	J	J	A	S	O	N	D
Goal 1	Reduce # of service calls/1000 users from 50/week to 25/week												
Goal 2	Improve training score from 3.2/5 to 4.0/5												
Goal 3	Improve ability to understand customer's needs - to be more proactive												
Goal 4	Achieve 20 implemented improvements												

IMPROVE - Implemented Improvements	CONTROL - 30 day check		CONTROL - 60 day check	
Fowarded all customer complaints to Tech Support	G			
Deleted unused apps from MaxPTs	G			
Updated training materials	G			
Taking course on insurance industry	G			

"This is the goal sheet I started for you. Each month you should assign a color to each of your goals. Green indicates it's on track. Those that have a yellow or red status require a plan to get it back on track."

"I like that. My goals are normally on a Post-it somewhere, so I like the idea of continually tracking them. Right now, I think all of my goals have a green, and we've quickly decreased customer complaints. I'm ready to send out the updated training session to the new Symbay department this week, and I've been going through the training materials from Justin to improve my ability to think strategically about my customers."

"I'm glad to hear that. How are you communicating your goals and their status with Justin?"

"We've been working well together. He's still a much different person than I am, but we've learned to speak in the same language. With that foundation, I have been letting him know what I want to achieve."

"It's important to review your goals and their status with Justin on a monthly basis."

They continued the conversation, evaluating the status of implemented and potential improvements.

"I guess this is the end of The 5 Disciplines, right?" Lauren asked.

"Well, you've learned all 5 steps, but The 5 Disciplines never ends. It's not a program; it's a systematic way to maximize your potential at every level in your career.

"Continue to think strategically, build your working relationships, and implement customer-centric improvements in a disciplined way," Claire explained.

"Once established, the *Define* and *Measure* steps remain constant throughout the year. To maximize improvements, you need to continually circle through *Analyze, Improve,* and *Control.* This is an annual process that starts over at the beginning of each year."

As Claire said, the *Control* step had been initiated, but would never be fully completed. Lauren would continue asking the control questions as she built her career. She looked forward to what she could achieve next.

• • • • •

With so much progress made on the Symbay account, Justin felt the rest of the Account Coordinators could benefit from learning how Lauren had implemented improvements. After Lauren had returned from her meeting with Claire, he stopped by her desk.

"Hi, Lauren. You've been doing such an amazing job with Symbay, would you be willing to lead a meeting with the other Account Coordinators to walk them through the process? I'd like you to lead the discussion to explore best practices and start standardizing some of the changes you've made."

Lauren wasn't sure she heard him right. Before, he hadn't trusted her to do her job without micromanaging her. Now he wanted her to lead a meeting with the entire department. She was thrilled.

"Of course! That would be great."

"Good, then I'll set something up for Friday," he said.

When he left, Lauren immediately began preparing. She knew how valuable The 5 Disciplines had been. Sharing it with the team would be a great way to introduce them to what she'd learned, and she could learn from their best practices. It would be a tremendous benefit to learn together. Friday couldn't come soon enough.

When it was time for the meeting, all five Account Coordinators settled into the conference room. It had been over a month since their last team meeting, so they were happy to be in the same room again.

Lauren began the meeting with a brief introduction, and then dove in. "Some of you may know we had some challenges with the Symbay account. They even considered looking for an alternative device and dropping the MaxPTs.

"Luckily, I learned about The 5 Disciplines of Highly Effective Employees. For the past couple months, I've been working through each step. It's allowed us to completely turn around the account and secure Symbay as a committed customer."

One of the Account Coordinators asked, "What are The 5 Disciplines?"

Lauren smiled. All of a sudden she realized she was in Claire's position, introducing The 5 Disciplines. She gave a brief overview and told the team how she'd begun to implement improvements.

"Our new COO, Claire, plans to provide 5 Disciplines training to all Account Coordinators. For now, I'd like to explain the improvements I've implemented and discuss how we can standardize them within our department. I'd also like to explore the solutions that other Account Coordinators have been using in their day-to-day operations. We won't be able to get into too much depth, but I'd like to at least open the dialogue. As The 5 Disciplines is implemented at Maximum Potential, we can continue working together with meetings like this."

Lauren began with the simplest improvement she'd made: updating her filing system. When she asked the team how they organized their files, they each had different methods. Lauren explained how this lack of standardization could cause waste, and it would be valuable for them to determine a shared organization system that would work for everyone.

Next, Lauren discussed the training material. When she asked, none of the Account Coordinators had customized training materials for clients. They were all using the one-size-fits-all manual Lauren had used two months ago that proved to be ineffective.

One member of the team spoke up. "It seems like it's a lot of information that isn't really helping customers."

"That's exactly what I found," Lauren responded. "Symbay, like each of your customers, uses the MaxPTs in a unique way. Providing information that wasn't relevant to them was leading to user errors."

The other Account Coordinators had experienced this same challenge. The training materials were too complex, which was leading to non-value added work. Lauren shared her updates and suggested each team member customize their training materials for the customer.

Lastly, Lauren reviewed the insight she'd gained about *the genius of the and*—You'll provide the most value by solving problems reactively AND proactively. She discussed the coaching she had received from Justin.

Two of the other Account Coordinators had used similar resources to hone their strategic thinking. One of them had found an online resource specifically created for employees in account services to consult with their customers.

Lauren was thrilled about the additional training resources. Perhaps it could help with her continuous improvement efforts.

Justin wrapped up the meeting by describing how he had seen The 5 Disciplines help Lauren and how invaluable he knew it would be for the rest of the team.

· · · · ·

The rest of the week continued smoothly. Lauren scheduled a meeting with Phillip to discuss the future needs of Symbay and how Maximum Potential could be a partner in achieving those needs. Lauren felt she was finally operating as a full Technical Account Manager.

When Saturday rolled around, she was excited for her daughter's birthday party.

Claire arrived first. She entered the chaos of the party with a big wrapped box in her arm.

"Let me help you with that!" Lauren said as she rushed over to Claire.

Lauren set the present down, and brought Claire a drink. They walked outside to the backyard where kids were playing and parents were chatting.

Lauren's conversation with Claire was interrupted by the doorbell. "Oh! Excuse me, while I get that," she said as she left Claire to mingle with the other guests.

She opened the door. "Hi, Justin! Glad you could come." She wanted to make him feel comfortable as he entered the party. She led him out to the backyard where Claire was seated.

"Well, this is the first time the three of us have been together," Lauren said with a smile.

They engaged in pleasant small talk until Claire took control of the conversation.

"I'm glad you're both here, because now would be the perfect time to share some good news," she said.

"Good news? This sounds exciting," Lauren responded. "Does this have something to do with the meeting you had with Symbay earlier this week?"

"As a matter of fact, it does. When I went to Symbay on Wednesday, I didn't just meet with Phillip. I met the founder of the company, Dr. Alexandra Henderson. After discussing the account for a bit, she told me they've been thoroughly impressed with the progress we've made and the way the devices are helping them achieve their business goals."

Lauren and Justin looked at each other, excited about the success they'd created for their customer, but that wasn't all Claire had to say.

"Specifically, they were so excited about how the MaxPTs helped engage employees, increase productivity, and improve customer satisfaction, they want to use the MaxPTs company-wide."

"What?" Lauren gasped in disbelief. "The whole company? That's huge."

"Yep, the whole company, from 500 users to 10,000. And you'll be managing the entire thing."

Lauren couldn't believe her ears. Only a couple months ago, Symbay had considered closing their account with Max Potential, but now they wanted to purchase a device for every Symbay employee.

Justin congratulated Lauren and began making plans to handle the new business.

"It's a birthday party; we can do the planning at work," Lauren thought to herself with an internal eye roll. But this time, she smiled because she knew it was just part of Justin's persistent and motivated attitude towards his work. And she couldn't wait to get started.

Claire said, "I truly believe this new business is a result of your engagement with your jobs. In the final analysis, the most important question you can ask yourself is: Are you engaged?"

Lauren stood back to watch as Claire and Justin talked about how to handle the new business. She looked out at the birthday party and her daughter running around the backyard with her friends. Without the stress she'd experienced two months ago, everything was more enjoyable. The 5 Disciplines had transformed her thinking and maximized her potential.

CONTROL STEP SUMMARY

The following questions can be asked in the *Control* step to help answer the question "*Am I maintaining the Gains?*"

Am I achieving my goals?

By reviewing your goals monthly, you can gauge your progress with The 5 Disciplines visual management system. The color codes of green, yellow, and red indicate status.

Lauren reviewed her goals.

- Goal 1: Reduce number of service calls from an average of 50 per week to 25 per week per 1000 users. The current rate of 35 represents a 30% reduction - yellow.

- Goal 2: Improve the training score from 2.5 to 4.0 out of 5. Currently there is no data on this - yellow.

- Goal 3: Improve ability to understand customer's needs in order to be more proactive. She didn't know how to determine the status of this goal. Claire suggested she qualitatively evaluate Goal 3 by writing down a set of improvements she thought would help the customer's business. No color yet.

- Goal 4: Twenty implemented improvements. So far, 17 implemented improvements - Green.

Am I communicating my goals/status with my manager?

Goals need to be reviewed monthly with your manager. During that time, both of you should agree upon green, yellow, and red designations. Goals that are color-coded yellow or red need a plan to achieve green status.

- Lauren reviewed her goals with Justin. Goal 1 and Goal 2 were in the green, but Goal 3 needed future action to be moved to green. Justin was pleased with her exceptional progress on Goal 4. Through open and honest communication, Lauren and Justin to made a mutually agreeable plan that would help her achieve green status for Goal 3.

Am I maintaining the gains achieved?

Once goals have been achieved, it is important to continue to monitor them to ensure you are not backsliding.

- Lauren's Goal 1 consistently stayed around 25 calls per week, plus or minus 5. Goal 2 was consistently above 4.03 out of 5.0. Claire was just beginning to coach Lauren on how to achieve Goal 3.

Am I staying organized?

It is difficult for anyone to continue to sustain long-term quality and productivity in any job without staying organized.

- Lauren implemented the 5S (Sort, Set and order, Shine, Standardize, and Sustain) process she learned from Justin.

Am I fully engaged?

Engaged means you care about the success of your department, organization, and its customers. You care so much that you want to bring your best effort and deliver improvements that will increase the productivity and quality of your department.

- Lauren was fully engaged in achieving her individual goals and helping achieve her department's goals through individual and team-based improvements.

SUMMARY

Our Mission is "To help organizations and the people who work there reach their full potential."

"The 5 Disciplines of Highly Effective Employees (Maximize YOUR Potential)" provides any employee with a systematic process to achieve their full potential. It is closely aligned to Dr. Deming's Plan Do Study Act cycle for continuous improvement and is a methodology that helps employees improve by asking the following five questions.

Define – *What is my job? - PLAN*

Measure – *Am I doing a good job? - PLAN*

Analyze – *How do I analyze my job? - PLAN*

Improve – *How do I improve? - DO*

Control – *Am I maintaining my gains? - STUDY & ACT*

However, this process alone cannot help an organization reach its full potential. In fact, "The 5 Disciplines of Highly Effective Employees" is part of a larger management system that includes "The 5 Disciplines of Highly Effective Managers" and "The 5 Disciplines of Highly Effective Executives".

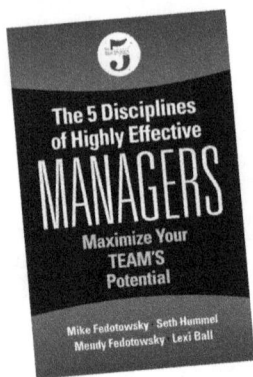

"The 5 Disciplines of Highly Effective Managers (Maximize your TEAM's Potential)" provides managers with a systematic process to achieve their department's full potential by helping people in their department align the goals for their specific job with the department's goals. This book will come out in 2018 and will focus on Justin as the main character. The following five questions will be the focus of Manager book.

Define – *What is our team's job? - PLAN*

Measure – *Are we doing a good job? - PLAN*

Analyze – *How do we analyze our job? - PLAN*

Improve – *How do we improve? - DO*

Control – *Are we maintaining our gains? – STUDY & ACT*

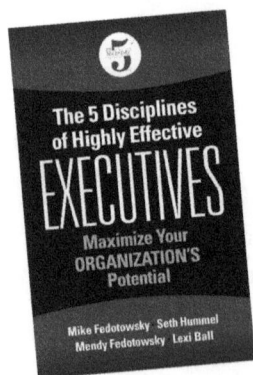

"The 5 Disciplines of Highly Effective Executives (Maximize your ORGANIZATION's Potential)" provides executives with a systematic process to achieve their organization's full potential by aligning everyone to the organization strategic and operational goals. This book will come out in 2019 and will focus on Claire as the main character. The following five questions will be the focus of the Executive book.

Define – *What is our business? - PLAN*

Measure – *Are we healthy? - PLAN*

Analyze – *How do we analyze our business? - PLAN*

Improve – *How do we improve? – DO*

Control – *Are we maintaining the gains? – STUDY & ACT*

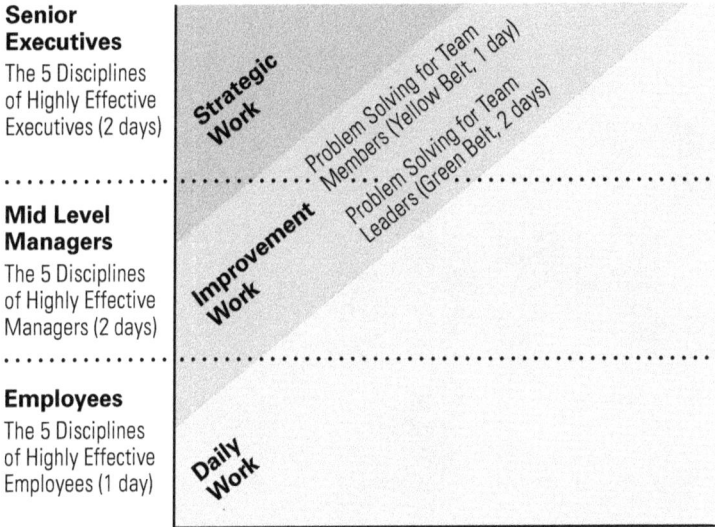

Our 5 training courses are depicted in the model below.

Senior Executives
The 5 Disciplines of Highly Effective Executives (2 days)

Mid Level Managers
The 5 Disciplines of Highly Effective Managers (2 days)

Employees
The 5 Disciplines of Highly Effective Employees (1 day)

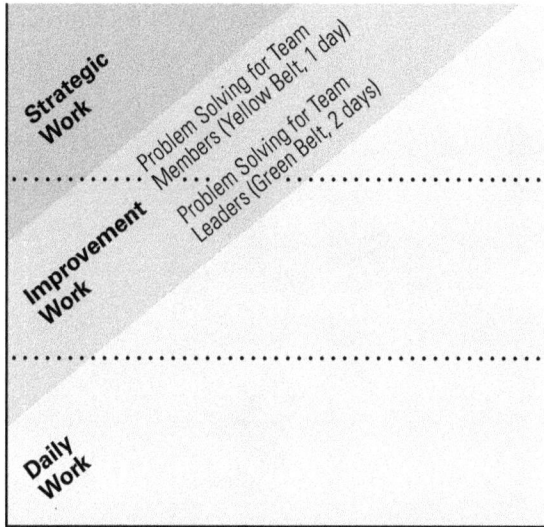

Strategic Work

Improvement Work

Daily Work

Problem Solving for Team Members (Yellow Belt, 1 day)

Problem Solving for Team Leaders (Green Belt, 2 days)

The above model helps explain how the overall system relates to the different types of work required by employees, managers and executives.

Daily Work is the perfect execution of standard work processes. It is the daily production of the products and services that the organization's customers use and experience.

Improvement Work is the ability of all employees to solve problems and continuously improve their work processes (that create the products and services for your customers).

Strategic Work is deciding the long-term direction of the organization. It is the planning that decides what products/services to offer to which customers and in what geographies.

Consulting and Training Contact

To discuss our Consulting and Training options and for a free Return on Investment analysis, please contact:

Seth Hummel
seth.h@the5disciplines.org

ABOUT THE AUTHORS

Mike Fedotowsky
While Mike has a Masters degree in Nuclear Physics, he certainly does not fit the profile. Since graduating, he quickly understood that he was better working with people than in a lab. He first realized this when helping Florida Power & Light become the first American company to earn the Deming Prize (Japan's National Award for Quality in honor of Dr. Deming). He was so valuable to the process of acquiring that prize, that they asked him to become a lead consultant for Qualtec; helping organizations implement the valuable process improvement techniques they learned from their Japanese consultants. He is an avid learner and is fascinated with what makes organizations work. Over the past 28 years as a consultant, his career has taken him all over the world; consulting for such companies as The Irish Management Institute, Eli Lilly France, Tube Makers Australia, Procter & Gamble, World Bank, CareSource and many others. Over the years, Mike has developed expertise incorporating the mantra "Simplify, Simplify, Simplify." Mike is known for his uncanny ability to decipher between value-added work and unnecessary fluff. The streamlined results have delighted his customers, improved morale and increased the bottom line. He has all the credentials; Qualtec Master's Trainer, Master Black Belt and Lean Ohio Certified Instructor, but he doesn't let that get in his way. He just wants to help organizations improve, innovate and lead in the most efficient way possible. He is the Co-Founder and CEO of The 5 Disciplines, Inc.

Seth Hummel
Seth is a hardworking, boot strapping entrepreneur who started his first business at the age of 12. When you first meet him, you quickly realize that his goal is an open and honest dialog to determine if the solutions his company offers are a perfect fit for you. If not, Seth is the first one to suggest solutions

other than his own. Seth truly wants to know what he can do to make you and your company better. The question of "How can I help you improve your life, your employees lives and help you sleep better at night?" is a typical question he might ask. Seth is a former 4th Grade teacher and coach who left the teaching profession to sell for his parents consulting company in 1997. Since then he has started nineteen businesses, four of which he sold, five that are still operating and ten that completely failed or fizzled out over time. Seth often notes that his business failures taught him more than the successes. He has a M.Ed. in Educational Leadership and has studied Business Process Design, Strategic Management, and Problem Solving at Massachusetts Institute of Technology (MIT) Sloan School of Management and the University of Dayton. He is the Co-Founder and CSO of The 5 Disciplines, Inc.

Mendy Fedotowsky

In the early 80's, Mendy began her career with PQ Systems, Inc., a company whose mission was to help companies implement the then unknown principles of "Quality Management." She was fortunate to be on the cusp of a management system that aligned with her own beliefs that employees have the best ideas if you simply ask them and give them a method for driving continuous improvement. She learned from the great pioneers of the movement, Deming, Juran, and others. Through the company's belief in professional development, Mendy became a certified Train-the-Trainer in the Total Quality Transformation; a training system for which she was also the project leader. Since that time, she's gone on to launch a successful business, develop her skills as a trainer and feed a passion for learning. She's witnessed many changes in the Quality Management world. Even the name has morphed into "Lean Six Sigma." The evolution to a practical, less statistical method for making improvements is appealing. Mendy would be the first to admit her weakness for statistics. She's more compelled by what makes employees tick and take joy in their work. Mendy's undergraduate and graduate work is in education and organizational development. But her greatest education comes from her work experience and continuous pursuit of learning.

Lexi Ball

When it was time to pick her major in college, Lexi knew three things—she didn't know what she wanted to do; when she figured out, she'd need to know how to think; and she'd need to understand people. So, she decided to study philosophy and psychology. In her senior year, she uncovered the path she wanted to pursue—writing. Without a portfolio and the typical education, she knew she'd have to take an unconventional path, so she found her way into strategy and account management. Her strategy in her new career was simple—work as hard as possible and learn just as much. By freelancing and sneaking her way into creative projects, Lexi had built the portfolio to get hired as a copywriting intern at LPK. There she worked on CPG brands and led rebranding projects for local non-profits, solidifying her hunch that the creative field was exactly where she needed to be. The internship ended and she finally found the job she'd been looking for—a copywriter at Hasbro writing for Transformers, Beyblade, and new business brands—developing story worlds and crafting messaging strategies. It was…epic. In every challenge, Lexi delivers a passionate enthusiasm for reaching people with meaningful messages. She believes in the power of story and hopes to someday create the next hit superhero world.